RACISTEM:
A Comprehensive Handbook for Dialoging Systemic Racism

Copyright © 2025 by Robert L. Gatewood.

All Rights Reserved. Printed in the United States of America. No part of this book may be sold, distributed, resold, hired out, or otherwise circulated without the publisher's prior permission except in the case of brief quotations included in critical reviews.

Duplicating or distributing this book by any means without the publisher's permission is not allowed. Only purchased copies of authorized editions that do not violate copyright laws are permitted.

First Edition, 2025 Gatewood Marketing, Inc.

ISBN- 979-8-218-72749-9

Introduction

America's story is inseparable from race. From founding to present, racial hierarchies have shaped institutions, policies, and lived experiences. This book examines the systemic nature of racial inequality, how it operates and how it persists despite legal and social progress.

Understanding racism as a system requires recognizing the historical, institutional, and cultural forces that maintain racial disparities even without explicit discriminatory intent. It means acknowledging how racial categories were constructed through law, science, religion, and culture to establish power hierarchies.

America's racial landscape reveals both the persistence of systemic racism and continuous resistance to it. From abolition to civil rights to contemporary movements, Americans have challenged the nation to fulfill its ideals of equality. These struggles have produced change while exposing how deeply embedded racism remains.

This exploration examines the contradictions, backlash, and resilience in the ongoing movement for equity. By understanding racism as operating across institutions, policies, cultural norms, and behaviors, we can recognize both its impacts and possibilities for transformation.

Confronting uncomfortable truths about American history and society is essential, not to assign blame or deflect accountability, but to create pathways toward justice. Understanding systemic racism ultimately aims to build a future where racial identity no longer determines life outcomes, and where America's promise of equality becomes reality for all.

Contents

Introduction 2
Systemic Racism Explained 5
Origins of Systemic Racism in the US 6
Individual, Institutional, and Systemic Racism 7
Structural Racism: Framework and Concept 10
The Psychological Toll of Systemic Racism 11
Everyday Microaggressions and Cultural Hostility 15
Child and Youth Outcomes 18
Intergenerational Trauma 21
Intersectionality: Gender & Immigration 23
Racialization of National Identity 26
Myths and Narratives Reinforcing Systemic Racism 28
Institutional Racism in Education 30
Higher Education and Representation Issues 32
Housing and Redlining 34
Impact on Homeownership and Wealth 36
Racism in Health Care 38
Criminal Justice System Bias 40
Policing and Mass Incarceration 42
Voting Rights and Representation 44
Embedded Racism in Law and Government 47
The Role of Policy in Perpetuating Racism 49
Military Service 51
Foreign Policy 54
Domestic Terrorism 55
Employment and Workplace Discrimination 58

Economic Opportunity and Inequality ... 60
Business and Entrepreneurship ... 62
Access to Capital and Banking ... 65
Media and Cultural Representation ... 68
Music Industry ... 70
Advertising and Media Buying ... 73
The Role of Religion and Faith Institutions ... 77
The Impact of Institutional Racism in STEMM ... 79
Environmental Racism ... 82
Native American Experiences ... 85
Latino and Immigrant Communities ... 88
Asian American Experience in the US System ... 91
Colorism and Internalized Oppression ... 94
How Systemic Racism Persists: Institutional Inertia ... 97
Data and the Measurement of Racial Inequities ... 100
Case Study: The Flint Water Crisis ... 103
Case Study: COVID-19 Pandemic Impacts ... 106
Myths Debunked: Progress and Remaining Barriers ... 109
The Role of Grassroots Activism ... 113
Government and Judicial Responses ... 117
Corporate America and DEI Initiatives ... 121
The Role of Education in Remediation ... 126
Pathways to Dismantling Systemic Racism ... 129
Call-to-Action: 10 Steps Towards a More Just and Equitable Nation ... 134
Glossary ... 137
Resources and References ... 156

Systemic Racism Explained

Racism in the United States transcends individual prejudice. For the purposes of this book, we inject the term "racistem," a portmanteau of "racism" and "system." This term serves to encapsulate systemic racism, highlighting how racial discrimination is intricately woven into the very fabric of American society in general, and the Black experience in particular.

Unlike isolated acts of bigotry, racistem and systemic racism refer to the complex network of embedded policies, practices, and cultural norms that work collectively to disadvantage racial and ethnic minority groups while preserving privileges for the dominant group.

At its core, systemic racism represents a pervasive force woven into the fabric of American society. It functions through laws, policies, institutional practices, and cultural representations that create and maintain racial disparities in virtually every aspect of American life. These disparities are not random or coincidental but rather the predictable results of systems designed—either intentionally or through accumulated effects—to privilege some while disadvantaging others based on racial categories.

The ubiquity of systemic racism in the United States can be observed across numerous domains: education, housing, criminal justice, healthcare, employment, wealth creation, environmental protection, and political representation. In each of these spheres, data consistently shows racial disparities that cannot be fully explained by factors other than structural discrimination and its intergenerational effects.

Understanding systemic racism has become increasingly relevant in contemporary debates about social justice, equity, and national identity. As events like the murder of George Floyd in 2020 and subsequent protests have demonstrated, confronting systemic racism requires acknowledging historical realities while examining present-day structures that perpetuate inequity. This examination must move beyond individual attitudes to address the systems and institutions that distribute resources, opportunities, and burdens unequally along racial lines.

Origins of Systemic Racism in the US

The roots of systemic racism in the United States extend deep into the nation's colonial past, beginning with the establishment of chattel slavery in the early 17th century. This system, which treated enslaved Africans as property rather than human beings, formed the economic foundation for much of the country's early development. By codifying racial hierarchy into law, colonial governments created the legal precedent for race-based discrimination that would influence American institutions for centuries to come.

The Constitution itself contained compromises that protected slavery, including the Three-Fifths Compromise and provisions for the return of fugitive slaves. Even after the Civil War and the abolition of slavery through the 13th Amendment, new systems of racial control emerged. The brief period of Reconstruction was followed by the implementation of Jim Crow laws across the South, establishing legal segregation and disenfranchisement of Black Americans that would last until the mid-20th century.

During the Jim Crow era (approximately 1877-1965), segregation was enforced in public facilities, schools, transportation, restrooms, restaurants, and housing. These laws were reinforced by Supreme Court decisions like Plessy v. Ferguson (1896), which established the "separate but equal" doctrine. The reality, however, was systematic inequality in the quality of facilities, educational resources, and opportunities available to Black Americans.

Beyond the South, de facto segregation and discrimination operated through less explicit but equally effective means, including restrictive covenants in housing, discriminatory hiring practices, and violence or intimidation against Black Americans who challenged the racial order. The Great Migration of Black Americans from the South to Northern and Western cities was met with new forms of segregation and discrimination in these urban centers.

This historical legacy of racial hierarchy established patterns that continue to shape contemporary American institutions. Understanding this history is essential to recognizing how systemic racism operates not merely as present-day discrimination but as the accumulated disadvantage produced by centuries of policies and practices designed to maintain racial stratification.

Individual, Institutional, and Systemic Racism

To fully comprehend racism in American society, it's essential to distinguish between its different manifestations: individual, institutional, and systemic. These forms of racism operate on different levels but interact with and reinforce one another to create comprehensive patterns of racial disadvantage.

Individual racism refers to personal prejudice, bias, or discrimination based on race. This includes explicit racial animus, conscious stereotyping, and unconscious bias that influences how individuals interact with people of different racial backgrounds. While this is the most visible and commonly recognized form of racism, focusing exclusively on personal prejudice obscures the broader structures that perpetuate racial inequality regardless of individual intentions.

Institutional racism operates at the level of specific organizations and institutions, manifesting in policies, practices, and procedures that disadvantage certain racial groups. Examples include disparate disciplinary practices in schools that disproportionately punish students of color, hiring processes that systematically exclude qualified minority candidates, or lending practices that deny mortgages to applicants from certain neighborhoods. These institutional patterns can persist even when individual members of the institution do not hold explicitly racist views.

Systemic racism encompasses the entire complex of social forces, institutions, ideologies, and processes that interact to maintain a racial hierarchy that allows privilege and power to be concentrated with the dominant group. It operates across multiple institutions simultaneously and throughout society as a whole. Systemic racism is reinforced by cultural myths and norms that rationalize racial inequality as the natural result of individual or group deficiencies rather than structural barriers.

Individual Level

- Personal prejudice and bias
- Explicit or implicit racial stereotypes
- Discriminatory interactions between individuals
- Microaggressions in daily encounters

Institutional Level

- Organizational policies with disparate racial impacts
- Workplace hiring and promotion practices
- School disciplinary procedures
- Banking and lending criteria

Systemic Level

- Interaction between multiple institutions
- Historical accumulation of disadvantage
- Cultural narratives justifying racial hierarchy
- Legal and political frameworks maintaining inequality

These different levels of racism often operate simultaneously and reinforce each other. For example, cultural stereotypes (system) may influence institutional policies in schools (institutional), which in turn shape how teachers interact with students of different races (individual). Understanding these distinctions helps reveal why addressing racism requires more than just changing individual attitudes—it demands transformation of institutions and systems.

Structural Racism: Framework and Concept

Structural racism provides a comprehensive framework for understanding how racial inequality is produced and maintained in American society. This concept extends beyond individual policies or institutional practices to encompass the totality of social, economic, and political structures that collectively generate racial disparities. Structural racism recognizes that these disparities are not accidental but rather the predictable result of systems designed—whether intentionally or through accumulated effect—to distribute resources and opportunities unequally along racial lines.

At its foundation, structural racism acknowledges the historical context from which current inequalities emerge. The present-day distribution of wealth, power, and opportunity cannot be understood without recognizing how systems like slavery, segregation, and discrimination have shaped access to resources over generations. These historical systems have created durable patterns of advantage and disadvantage that persist even after explicit discrimination has been outlawed.

What distinguishes structural racism from other frameworks is its emphasis on the interconnection between various domains of society. Housing discrimination, for instance, affects educational opportunities through school segregation, which influences employment prospects, which impacts health outcomes and wealth accumulation. These mutually reinforcing systems create a web of disadvantage that is difficult to escape even with individual effort or achievement.

The reproduction of racial inequality across generations is a key component of structural racism. Through mechanisms like residential segregation, school funding disparities, discriminatory lending, and intergenerational wealth transfer, racial advantages and disadvantages are passed down from parents to children. This process occurs regardless of whether current participants in these systems hold explicitly racist views.

Understanding structural racism also helps explain why racial disparities persist despite formal legal equality. Even "race-neutral" policies can produce racially disparate outcomes when implemented within existing structures of inequality. For example, college admissions criteria that appear neutral may nonetheless disadvantage students from under-resourced schools that serve predominantly minority communities.

By focusing on structures rather than individuals, this framework shifts attention from intentions to outcomes, from assigning blame to identifying systemic solutions. Addressing structural racism requires transformative changes to fundamental aspects of American society rather than simply punishing individual discriminatory acts or implementing superficial diversity initiatives.

The Psychological Toll of Systemic Racism

The psychological impact of racism extends to identity development, particularly for children and adolescents. Young people of color must navigate complex questions of belonging and self-definition in a society that often devalues their racial identities. Research indicates that strong, positive racial identity can serve as a protective factor against the psychological harms of discrimination, but developing such identity requires supportive environments and positive representations that are not equally available to all youth.

Beyond tangible disparities in resources and opportunities, systemic racism exacts a profound psychological toll on individuals and communities. These mental and emotional impacts represent a significant dimension of racial inequality, affecting health outcomes, identity formation, and overall well-being for people of color in ways that are often overlooked in discussions of systemic racism.

Research consistently documents higher rates of psychological distress among racial minorities exposed to discrimination. Experiences of racism—whether overt harassment or more subtle forms of exclusion—trigger stress responses and can lead to conditions including anxiety, depression, and post-traumatic stress disorder. A 2018 meta-analysis found that perceived discrimination was associated with increased depressive and anxiety symptoms, with stronger effects when discrimination was based on race rather than other characteristics.

Racial Battle Fatigue

This is the cumulative psychological wear caused by constant vigilance against potential discrimination and microaggressions. People of color often describe the mental exhaustion of navigating predominantly white spaces where they must constantly monitor their behavior, appearance, and speech to avoid triggering negative stereotypes or unwanted attention. This hypervigilance consumes cognitive resources that might otherwise be directed toward educational, professional, or personal goals.

Internalized Racism

The acceptance of negative societal messages about one's racial group—represents another psychological consequence of systemic racism. When consistently exposed to negative stereotypes and devaluation, individuals may begin to accept these characterizations as valid, leading to diminished self-esteem and restricted sense of possibility. This psychological process can manifest in various ways: rejection of cultural practices or physical characteristics associated with one's racial group; distancing from other members of one's racial group; setting lower expectations for oneself based on stereotypes; or engaging in self-sabotaging behaviors that confirm negative stereotypes. Research demonstrates connections between internalized racism and depression, anxiety, substance use, and reduced academic performance.

Racial Trauma

The cumulative psychological injury resulting from racist encounters produces symptoms similar to post-traumatic stress disorder, including hypervigilance, intrusive thoughts, avoidance behaviors, and emotional numbing. Unlike isolated traumatic events, racial trauma typically involves ongoing exposure without opportunity for complete recovery. The anticipatory stress of expecting discrimination in various settings creates additional psychological burden. For example, studies document physiological stress responses in Black patients before medical appointments, reflecting anxiety about potential mistreatment in healthcare settings. This chronic activation of stress responses consumes cognitive and emotional resources that could otherwise be directed toward education, career advancement, relationships, and other aspects of wellbeing.

Stereotype Threat

The fear of confirming negative stereotypes about one's group—creates additional psychological barriers in achievement contexts. When racial stereotypes about intellectual ability are made salient, individuals from stereotyped groups typically perform worse on cognitive tasks despite equal ability. This effect has been documented in laboratory settings and real-world contexts including standardized testing, where it contributes to persistent achievement gaps. The cognitive load of suppressing anxiety and monitoring performance for stereotype confirmation consumes working memory capacity needed for the task itself. This phenomenon demonstrates how awareness of systemic racism affects performance independent of actual ability, creating psychological barriers to achievement even in the absence of explicit discrimination in the immediate environment.

Healing Spaces

Culturally responsive mental health services can help address the psychological effects of racial trauma and build resilience.

Community Resilience

Collective healing practices and cultural affirmation serve as protective factors against the psychological harms of racism.

Mental health services often fail to adequately address these race-related stressors. Cultural mismatches between predominantly white providers and clients of color can limit the effectiveness of treatment, while stigma surrounding mental health in some communities of color creates additional barriers to care. Many standard therapeutic approaches do not explicitly address the role of racism in psychological distress, potentially leaving a significant source of trauma unaddressed.

Addressing the psychological toll of racism requires multilevel interventions: increasing racial diversity among mental health providers, developing culturally responsive treatment approaches, creating affirming spaces within institutions, and ultimately reducing discriminatory experiences through structural change. By recognizing psychological harm as a significant dimension of racial inequality, we can better understand the comprehensive impact of systemic racism on human lives and well-being.

Everyday Microaggressions and Cultural Hostility

While discussions of systemic racism often focus on formal policies and measurable disparities, the daily lived experience of racism frequently takes the form of microaggressions—subtle, often unintentional slights, snubs, insults or stereotypes that communicate hostile, derogatory, or negative messages to people based on their racial identity. These brief, pedestrian indignities may seem minor in isolation but cumulatively create an environment of cultural hostility that reinforces racial hierarchies and exacts a significant psychological toll.

Racial microaggressions take various forms. "Microassaults" are explicit racial derogations, such as using racial slurs or displaying racist symbols. "Microinsults" are communications that subtly convey rudeness or insensitivity, such as expressing surprise at a person of color's articulateness or professional success. "Microinvalidations" dismiss or negate the experiences of people of color, such as claims of colorblindness that deny the reality of racial difference or assertions that racism is no longer significant. Each type communicates that people of color are somehow deficient, deviant, or not belonging.

Common microaggressions in educational settings include mispronouncing or avoiding non-Anglo names, low expectations for academic performance from students of color, curriculum that excludes diverse perspectives, and disproportionate scrutiny of minority students' behavior. Black students report being mistaken for service workers on campus, having their presence questioned in academic spaces, and being treated as representatives of their entire race during classroom discussions about race.

In workplace contexts, microaggressions include being mistaken for administrative staff regardless of position, having ideas ignored until repeated by white colleagues, receiving excessive scrutiny of work products, and experiencing "tokenism" where individuals are expected to represent their entire racial group. Comments about being "articulate" or "not like other" members of one's racial group, while often intended as compliments, communicate that the person is an exception to presumed racial deficiencies.

Identity Questioning

"Where are you really from?" or "What are you?" questions that imply perpetual foreignness regardless of citizenship or birth

Unwanted Touching

Touching hair or commenting on physical features in ways that objectify and exoticize racial differences

Surveillance

Excessive monitoring in stores or public spaces based on racial stereotypes about criminality

Ascription of Intelligence

Assumptions about intellectual capability based solely on racial identity

Denial of Experience

Dismissing accounts of racism with responses like "you're being too sensitive" or "playing the race card"

Technological environments also feature microaggressions, from facial recognition software that works less effectively on darker skin tones to voice recognition systems that struggle with non-standard accents. These technological failures communicate that the default user is white, while other users must adapt to systems not designed with their characteristics in mind.

The impact of these everyday experiences is cumulative and significant. Research links exposure to microaggressions with increased symptoms of depression, anxiety, and traumatic stress. The constant vigilance required to navigate environments where microaggressions are common depletes cognitive resources that might otherwise be directed toward learning, work, or creativity.

Social belonging and institutional trust are undermined by repeated subtle messages of exclusion.

Addressing microaggressions requires both individual awareness and institutional change. Education about the nature and impact of microaggressions, creating mechanisms for reporting and addressing incidents, and developing inclusive cultural norms all contribute to more equitable environments. However, meaningful change requires recognizing that microaggressions are not simply interpersonal misunderstandings but rather manifestations of broader systemic racism that must be addressed at structural levels.

Child and Youth Outcomes

Achievement Gaps

Racial disparities in educational outcomes begin before kindergarten and persist through higher education. By age 3, white children typically have vocabularies twice the size of their Black and Hispanic peers, reflecting differences in early learning environments related to parental education, income, and neighborhood resources. These early gaps widen throughout the educational trajectory. By 12th grade, Black and Latino students are, on average, four years behind their white peers in academic achievement.

These disparities reflect systemic differences in educational opportunity rather than ability. Students of color are less likely to have access to high-quality preschool, experienced teachers, advanced courses, and well-resourced schools. Tracking practices disproportionately place students of color in lower-level courses even when they demonstrate similar achievement as white peers placed in advanced courses.

Discipline Disparities

School discipline shows stark racial disparities that begin in preschool and continue through K-12 education. Black children represent 18% of preschool enrollment but 48% of preschool children receiving multiple suspensions. In K-12 settings, Black students are 3.8 times more likely to receive suspensions than white students for similar behaviors. Native American students face the second-highest rates of discipline.

These disciplinary practices remove students from educational settings, contributing to academic disengagement and increased likelihood of dropping out. The presence of police officers in schools increases the likelihood that minor infractions will result in arrests and juvenile justice involvement, creating what educators term the "school-to-prison pipeline" that disproportionately affects students of color.

Housing segregation and environmental factors create additional barriers to healthy development for children of color. Residential patterns expose children of color to higher rates of environmental toxins, including lead, which causes irreversible cognitive damage. Black children are twice as likely as white children to have elevated blood lead levels, reflecting both older housing stock and proximity to industrial pollution. Access to safe outdoor play spaces, nutritious, and healthcare services shows similar disparities by neighborhood racial composition. These environmental factors affect both physical development and educational readiness.

The cumulative psychological impact of experiencing systemic racism creates additional developmental challenges. Children as young as 3-5 years old demonstrate awareness of racial stereotypes and begin experiencing their effects. By adolescence, youth of color report high rates of racial discrimination from peers, teachers, store employees, and law enforcement. Experiences of discrimination correlate with increased symptoms of depression, anxiety, substance use, and risky behaviors.

Weathering

Research demonstrates that the chronic stress of racial discrimination accelerates cellular aging and contributes to health disparities even in childhood and adolescence. These outcomes demonstrate how racistem affects children and youth across multiple domains, creating cumulative disadvantage that shapes life trajectories from the earliest stages of development.

The psychological impact of experiencing systemic racism creates significant burdens for people of color beyond the material disadvantages previously discussed. Chronic stress resulting from both overt discrimination and subtle microaggressions triggers physiological responses that, over time, contribute to health disparities. This "weathering" effect accelerates cellular aging through mechanisms including elevated cortisol levels, inflammation, and telomere shortening. These biological processes help explain why people of color show earlier onset and higher rates of stress-related conditions including hypertension, diabetes, and cardiovascular disease, even when controlling for socioeconomic status and health behaviors.

Intergenerational Trauma

Historical Trauma

Collective psychological injury inflicted on a group through historical events: enslavement, genocide, forced relocation, cultural erasure

Intergenerational Transmission

Transfer of trauma effects to subsequent generations through biological, psychological, and social mechanisms

Contemporary Manifestations

Ongoing expression of historical trauma through health disparities, cultural disconnection, psychological distress, and socioeconomic challenges

Intergenerational trauma resulting from systemic racism operates through multiple pathways. Emerging research in epigenetics suggests that extreme stress can cause changes in gene expression that may be passed to subsequent generations, potentially explaining some health disparities that persist across generations. While this research remains developing, more established mechanisms include psychological transmission through parenting practices and family narratives, socioeconomic inheritance of disadvantage, and ongoing exposure to similar traumatic stressors across generations.

Historical trauma manifests differently across racial groups based on specific histories of oppression. For Native Americans, forced relocation, boarding schools that separated children from families and prohibited cultural practices, and genocidal violence created profound community and cultural disruption. The effects continue through elevated rates of depression, substance abuse, suicide, and domestic violence in Native communities. For Black Americans, the traumas of enslavement, lynching, segregation, and ongoing police violence create a collective historical burden. Latino communities carry historical traumas related to colonization, territorial conquest, and cyclical targeting through immigration enforcement. Asian American groups face distinct historical traumas including exclusion laws, internment, refugee experiences, and periodic waves of anti-Asian violence.

Parenting in the context of systemic racism involves complex psychological challenges that affect intergenerational patterns. Parents of color must prepare children for potential discrimination while fostering positive racial identity and avoiding transmission of their own racial trauma. This "racial socialization" process requires significant psychological resources and emotional labor. Parental experiences of discrimination correlate with symptoms of depression and anxiety that can affect parenting capacity and parent-child attachment. Financial stress resulting from employment discrimination further strains family relationships and limits resources available for child development. These patterns demonstrate how racism affects not only individuals but family systems across generations.

Breaking cycles of intergenerational trauma requires both individual healing and structural change. Cultural reconnection, collective memory work, and trauma-informed mental health services can address psychological dimensions of historical trauma. However, these approaches prove insufficient without addressing ongoing structural sources of trauma, including discriminatory policies and practices that continue to reproduce racial disadvantage. The persistence of intergenerational trauma thus reveals the interconnection between historical injustice and contemporary systemic racism, highlighting the need for comprehensive approaches that address both past harms and present systems.

Intersectionality: Gender & Immigration

The concept of intersectionality, first articulated by legal scholar Kimberlé Crenshaw, recognizes that individuals experience multiple, overlapping forms of oppression or privilege based on their various social identities. Rather than examining race, gender, class, immigration status, sexuality, or disability in isolation, intersectionality explores how these identities interact to create unique experiences of discrimination or advantage. This framework is essential for understanding the complex ways systemic racism affects diverse individuals within racial groups.

Black women experience distinct forms of discrimination at the intersection of racism and sexism. In employment, Black women face both the racial wage gap and the gender wage gap, earning approximately 63 cents for every dollar earned by white men. In healthcare, Black women experience dramatically higher maternal mortality rates—three to four times those of white women—reflecting the combined effects of racial bias in medical treatment and gender-specific health needs. Social stereotypes about Black women, such as the "angry Black woman" trope, create unique forms of bias that differ from those experienced by either Black men or white women.

Immigration status creates another critical intersection with race. Latino immigrants face both xenophobia related to their immigrant status and racism based on their ethnicity or race. This intersection is evident in immigration enforcement practices that disproportionately target Latino communities, regardless of legal status, and in political rhetoric that racializes immigration by focusing on the U.S.-Mexico border while giving less attention to other sources of immigration. Asian immigrants encounter the "perpetual foreigner" stereotype that questions their American identity regardless of how long they or their families have been in the United States.

Class status significantly modifies experiences of racism. While middle-class and affluent people of color have greater resources to buffer some effects of discrimination, they often face distinct challenges like "belonging uncertainty" in professional or educational spaces, heightened expectations to represent their entire race, and being perceived as exceptions to racial stereotypes rather than evidence that the stereotypes are false. Meanwhile, low-income people of color face the combined effects of racial discrimination and economic marginalization, with limited resources to challenge or escape discriminatory systems.

Religion creates additional intersections, particularly for Muslims, Sikhs, and Jews of color who may experience both racism and religious discrimination. Muslim women who wear hijab, for instance, face particularly visible markers of difference that can trigger both racist and Islamophobic harassment. Indigenous peoples navigate unique intersections of racial identity, tribal sovereignty, and historical trauma from colonization that differ from other racial minority experiences.

Black Women

- Wage gap of 63% compared to white men
- 3-4 times higher maternal mortality rate
- Disproportionate school discipline rates
- Unique stereotypes affecting treatment

Immigrants of Color

- Profiling by immigration enforcement
- "Perpetual foreigner" stereotypes
- Language discrimination
- Limited access to services and benefits

Disability intersects with race in healthcare, education, and criminal justice. People of color with disabilities face compound discrimination in diagnosis, with conditions often misidentified or untreated. In education, Black students with disabilities are disproportionately subjected to harsh disciplinary measures. The criminal justice system disproportionately incarcerates people of color with mental illnesses, often providing inadequate treatment.

An intersectional approach to addressing systemic racism requires policies and interventions that recognize these complex interactions rather than treating all members of racial groups as having identical experiences. It means designing programs that address the specific needs of subgroups, collecting disaggregated data to identify patterns of inequality within racial categories, and ensuring that anti-racism efforts include diverse voices from all intersections of identity. By understanding how various forms of discrimination interact and compound one another, we can develop more effective and inclusive approaches to dismantling systemic racism.

Racialization of National Identity

The concept of American identity has been racialized since the nation's founding, with whiteness implicitly and explicitly positioned as a prerequisite for full citizenship and belonging. The Naturalization Act of 1790 restricted naturalized citizenship to "free white persons," codifying the racial boundaries of American identity in law. This racial definition persisted through subsequent immigration and naturalization policies, creating a legal framework that defined some racial groups as perpetually foreign regardless of birthplace or cultural assimilation. The Supreme Court's decisions in cases like Ozawa v. United States (1922) and United States v. Thind (1923) rejected citizenship applications from Japanese and Indian immigrants explicitly on racial grounds, reinforcing the equation of American identity with whiteness.

Cultural representations further reinforce the racialization of American identity. Media depictions of "typical Americans" or "heartland values" overwhelmingly feature white individuals and families, positioning whiteness as the unmarked norm and other racial identities as variations requiring qualification (African American, Asian American, etc.). Historical narratives emphasize European immigration and westward expansion while minimizing indigenous presence and contributions from other racial groups. National symbols and celebrations frequently center experiences and perspectives associated with white Americans, from Thanksgiving narratives that romanticize colonial settlement to Memorial Day commemorations that inadequately recognize military service by people of color.

Immigration discourse reveals particularly explicit racialization of national belonging. Political rhetoric frequently positions immigrants from predominantly white countries as unproblematically assimilable, while characterizing immigrants from Africa, Latin America, and parts of Asia as threats to national identity and cohesion. The consistent framing of immigration from Mexico and Central America as a "crisis" or "invasion" contrasts sharply with discussions of European immigration. Even immigrants who fully adopt American cultural practices and values face questioning of their American identity when they are not white, revealing how racialization persists independently of cultural assimilation.

This racialization affects civic participation and psychological belonging among Americans of color. Studies demonstrate that experiences of being treated as a foreigner or having one's American identity questioned correlate with reduced civic engagement, including voting and other forms of political participation. The psychological burden of constantly negotiating challenges to belonging creates an additional barrier to full citizenship in practice, regardless of legal status. For Indigenous peoples, the racialization of American identity creates particular contradictions, as they simultaneously face questioning of their American identity despite their nations' prior claim to the land now constituting the United States. These patterns demonstrate how the racialization of national identity functions as a mechanism of exclusion that maintains racial hierarchy by determining who is perceived as a legitimate member of the national community.

Myths and Narratives Reinforcing Systemic Racism

Cultural myths, narratives, and language play a powerful role in legitimizing and perpetuating systemic racism. These ideological elements provide the cognitive frameworks through which people interpret racial disparities, often in ways that naturalize inequality and obscure structural causes. By examining these myths and narratives, we can better understand how racism is maintained not just through formal institutions but through shared cultural understandings.

Language itself carries embedded racial hierarchies that shape perception from early childhood. Common expressions like "white lie" (harmless) versus "black mark" (negative), or "white knight" (savior) versus "black sheep" (outcast) subtly reinforce associations between whiteness and positive qualities, blackness and negative ones. The normalization of phrases like "sold down the river" or "grandfathered in"—terms with direct connections to slavery and Jim Crow voting restrictions—demonstrates how racial hierarchies become embedded in everyday communication.

American narratives of individualism and meritocracy often function to obscure systemic barriers. The myth that success is determined solely by hard work and personal responsibility attributes racial disparities to individual or cultural deficiencies rather than structural inequality. This framework suggests that those who haven't "succeeded" simply haven't worked hard enough, ignoring the uneven playing field created by historical and ongoing discrimination. The "bootstraps" narrative that anyone can pull themselves up through individual effort alone disregards how systemic advantages and disadvantages shape opportunities.

The Myth of Racial Progress

The narrative that racial equality has largely been achieved after the Civil Rights Movement minimizes ongoing disparities and suggests that remaining inequalities must be due to individual choices rather than structural barriers.

Media Stereotypes

Portrayals of Black men as criminals, Latinos as illegal immigrants, Asian Americans as perpetual foreigners, and Native Americans as historical relics rather than contemporary peoples reinforce dehumanizing stereotypes that justify discriminatory treatment.

Educational Omissions

Historical narratives that minimize or misrepresent slavery, genocide of Native peoples, and other racial injustices while celebrating narratives of American exceptionalism create distorted understandings of how race has shaped the nation.

The concept of colorblindness—the idea that the best way to address racism is to ignore race entirely—has become a powerful narrative that often works to maintain rather than challenge racial hierarchies. By suggesting that acknowledging race is itself problematic, colorblindness prevents recognition of how race continues to structure opportunity and disadvantage. This framework makes it difficult to identify or address systemic racism, as patterns of racial disparity become invisible or are attributed to non-racial factors.

These myths and narratives are perpetuated through education, media, political discourse, and everyday conversation. They function as powerful tools for maintaining the status quo by providing explanatory frameworks that justify racial inequality without requiring acknowledgment of racism. Challenging these narratives is therefore a crucial component of addressing systemic racism, requiring critical examination of the stories we tell about race, success, and American history.

Institutional Racism in Education

Education has long been heralded as the great equalizer in American society, yet the educational system frequently reinforces rather than remedies racial inequality. Institutional racism in education operates through multiple mechanisms—from funding disparities to curriculum design to disciplinary practices—creating an uneven playing field that systematically disadvantages students of color.

Perhaps the most fundamental educational inequality stems from school funding disparities. Because public schools are primarily funded through local property taxes, schools in wealthy areas receive substantially more resources than those in low-income communities. This seemingly race-neutral policy has profound racial implications due to residential segregation: the average non-white school district receives approximately $2,226 less per student than predominantly white districts. These funding gaps translate directly into differences in teacher salaries, class sizes, extracurricular offerings, technology access, and building quality.

Curriculum and pedagogical practices often reflect and reinforce racial hierarchies. History textbooks frequently minimize the brutality of slavery, glorify colonization, and underrepresent the contributions of people of color to American society. The literary canon remains predominantly white and male, while culturally responsive teaching practices that benefit diverse student populations are inconsistently implemented. Tracking systems that sort students into different academic levels disproportionately place students of color in lower tracks, even when controlling for prior academic performance.

Disciplinary practices reveal some of the starkest racial disparities in education. Black students are suspended and expelled at rates far higher than their white peers for similar behaviors. According to Department of Education data, Black students are nearly four times as likely to receive out-of-school suspensions as white students. These disparities begin in preschool, where Black children represent 18% of enrollment but 48% of children receiving multiple out-of-school suspensions. This "school-to-prison pipeline" pushes students of color out of educational opportunities and into contact with the criminal justice system.

Higher education perpetuates these inequalities. Historically Black Colleges and Universities (HBCUs) have been systematically underfunded compared to predominantly white institutions. Legacy admissions policies at elite universities give preference to children of alumni, a practice that benefits white applicants disproportionately given historical exclusion of people of color. Meanwhile, attacks on affirmative action have reduced efforts to remedy historical discrimination, while standardized testing requirements that correlate strongly with socioeconomic status create additional barriers.

These educational inequalities have profound long-term consequences, affecting college attendance, career opportunities, income potential, and even health outcomes. By systematically providing different educational experiences to students based largely on race and socioeconomic status, the American educational system becomes a key mechanism for reproducing racial inequality across generations rather than fulfilling its promise as a pathway to opportunity for all.

Higher Education and Representation Issues

Despite significant progress over the past several decades, higher education remains a domain where racial disparities persist in access, completion rates, experiences, and representation. These inequalities limit opportunities for social mobility and perpetuate racial gaps in income, wealth, and professional advancement.

Access to higher education continues to be stratified by race and ethnicity. While college enrollment rates have increased across all racial groups, substantial gaps remain. According to the National Center for Education Statistics, the immediate college enrollment rate for white high school graduates in 2019 was 69%, compared to 63% for Black graduates and 63% for Hispanic graduates. These disparities become even more pronounced at selective institutions, where Black and Latino students are significantly underrepresented relative to their share of the population.

Multiple barriers contribute to these access disparities. The rising cost of college hits communities of color particularly hard due to historical wealth gaps that limit families' ability to save for education. The average Black and Hispanic or Latino families have just a fraction of the wealth of the average white family, making it more difficult to afford tuition without taking on substantial debt. Financial aid policies that have shifted from need-based grants to loans and merit scholarships often disadvantage students from under-resourced schools, who are disproportionately students of color.

Even when students of color gain access to higher education, they face additional challenges to completion. Six-year graduation rates show significant racial disparities: 74% for Asian students, 64% for white students, 54% for Hispanic students, and 40% for Black students. These completion gaps reflect a complex interplay of factors, including greater financial pressures, experiences of discrimination and alienation on predominantly white campuses, and varying levels of academic preparation due to K-12 educational inequities.

Faculty and administrative leadership in higher education remains disproportionately white relative to both the student body and the general population. As of 2018, only 24% of full-time faculty members at degree-granting institutions were people of color, with particularly severe underrepresentation of Black and Hispanic faculty. This lack of representation affects mentorship opportunities for students of color, curriculum development, research priorities, and institutional policies.

Addressing racial inequities in higher education requires comprehensive approaches, including increasing financial support for students of color, reforming admissions processes to recognize diverse forms of merit, creating more inclusive campus climates, diversifying faculty and leadership, and strengthening the pipeline from K-12 education to college completion. Without such interventions, higher education may continue to function as a mechanism that reproduces rather than reduces racial inequality.

Housing and Redlining

Housing discrimination has been one of the most powerful mechanisms for creating and maintaining racial inequality in the United States. At the center of this system was the practice of redlining—the systematic denial of mortgages, insurance, and other financial services to residents of specific neighborhoods, primarily based on their racial composition. While redlining is often discussed as a historical practice, its effects continue to shape American communities and create barriers to wealth accumulation for families of color.

The federal government played a central role in institutionalizing housing discrimination. In the 1930s, the Home Owners' Loan Corporation (HOLC) created residential security maps for cities across the country, grading neighborhoods from "A" (green, "best") to "D" (red, "hazardous"). These grades were explicitly based on racial composition, with neighborhoods containing any significant number of Black residents invariably receiving "D" ratings regardless of the homes' actual conditions or the residents' economic status. The Federal Housing Administration (FHA), established in 1934, used these maps to determine eligibility for mortgage insurance, effectively refusing to back loans in redlined areas.

This federal policy was compounded by private discrimination. Banks used the HOLC maps to deny loans in redlined neighborhoods, a practice known as "redlining." Realtors engaged in "steering," directing white homebuyers away from integrated neighborhoods while restricting Black homebuyers to already-segregated areas. Restrictive covenants—legal clauses in property deeds that prohibited sale to non-white buyers—were common until the Supreme Court ruled them unenforceable in 1948, though informal versions persisted much longer.

The Fair Housing Act of 1968 outlawed explicit housing discrimination, but more subtle forms continued. Studies using paired testers consistently find that Black and Latino home-seekers are shown fewer properties, quoted higher prices, and denied financing more often than equally qualified white counterparts. Subprime lending leading up to the 2008 financial crisis disproportionately targeted communities of color, even when controlling for income and credit scores, leading to devastating foreclosure rates that erased decades of wealth accumulation.

The legacy of redlining and housing discrimination persists in stark residential segregation. A 2021 Brookings Institution analysis found that neighborhoods that were redlined in the 1930s remain significantly more likely to be home to lower-income residents and people of color today. These neighborhoods typically have lower home values, fewer amenities, more environmental hazards, and lower-performing schools—all factors that continue to limit opportunity for residents.

This history of housing discrimination has had profound intergenerational consequences. Because home equity represents the largest component of wealth for most American families, the systematic denial of homeownership opportunities has been a primary driver of the racial wealth gap. By understanding redlining not just as a historical practice but as a system whose effects continue to shape communities today, we can better appreciate how housing policy remains a critical site for addressing systemic racism.

Impact on Homeownership and Wealth

The consequences of housing discrimination extend far beyond where people live, profoundly shaping economic opportunities and intergenerational wealth transfer. Homeownership represents the primary wealth-building vehicle for most American families, and systemic barriers to property ownership have created one of the most persistent and substantial manifestations of racial inequality in the United States: the racial wealth gap.

The Black-white homeownership gap remains stubbornly wide. According to the U.S. Census Bureau, as of 2021, approximately 74% of white households owned their homes, compared to just 45% of Black households, 48% of Hispanic households, and 60% of Asian households. This 29-percentage-point gap between Black and white homeownership rates is actually wider today than it was in 1960, before the Fair Housing Act made housing discrimination illegal.

Even when people of color do achieve homeownership, they often face additional barriers to building equity. Homes in predominantly Black neighborhoods are consistently undervalued compared to similar properties in predominantly white areas. A 2018 Brookings Institution study found that homes in majority-Black neighborhoods are valued at approximately 23% less than comparable homes in neighborhoods with few or no Black residents, amounting to $48,000 per home on average. This devaluation of Black-owned property represents approximately $156 billion in lost equity.

These disparities in homeownership and home valuation contribute significantly to the racial wealth gap. According to Federal Reserve data, the median white family has approximately $171,000 in wealth, compared to just $17,600 for the median Black family and $20,700 for the median Hispanic family. This means the typical white family has nearly ten times the wealth of the typical Black family—a gap that has barely changed since the civil rights era.

The wealth gap has profound implications across generations. Wealth provides a safety net during economic hardship, enables investment in education and entrepreneurship, and can be passed down to children and grandchildren. Families with limited wealth have fewer resources to help the next generation with college costs, down payments on homes, or business startups, thereby perpetuating economic disadvantage across generations.

Housing policy remains a critical site for addressing these disparities. Potential interventions include strengthening enforcement of fair housing laws, implementing reparations programs, expanding first-time homebuyer assistance targeted at historically excluded communities, addressing bias in appraisals and lending, and investing in community development in previously redlined neighborhoods. Without deliberate policy action, the legacy of historical housing discrimination will continue to reproduce racial economic inequality for generations to come.

Racism in Health Care

The American healthcare system exhibits profound racial disparities that affect both access to care and health outcomes. These disparities reflect a complex interplay of socioeconomic factors, environmental conditions, and direct discrimination within healthcare settings. These are all manifestations of systemic racism that literally determine who lives and who dies in the United States.

Access to quality healthcare remains unequal along racial lines. People of color are significantly more likely to be uninsured or underinsured than white Americans. According to Census Bureau data, in 2020, the uninsured rate was 5.4% for non-Hispanic whites, compared to 10.4% for Black Americans, 18.3% for Hispanics, and 15.6% for American Indians and Alaska Natives. Even with insurance, geographic distribution of healthcare facilities often results in "medical deserts" in many predominantly minority communities, requiring longer travel times to reach providers and creating barriers to preventive care.

Even when access barriers are overcome, research consistently documents disparities in the quality of care received. Studies have shown that Black and Latino patients are less likely to receive pain medication, less likely to receive appropriate cardiac care, and more likely to have necessary procedures delayed compared to white patients with identical symptoms and insurance status.

These disparities reflect both explicit bias and implicit stereotypes among healthcare providers that affect clinical decision-making.

The consequences of these disparities are evident in health outcomes. Black Americans face higher rates of maternal mortality, resulting in Black women being three to four times more likely to die from pregnancy-related causes than white women. Life expectancy for Black Americans is consistently lower than for white Americans, with the gap widening during the COVID-19 pandemic. Native Americans have the highest diabetes rates of any racial group, while Black Americans face higher rates of hypertension, heart disease, and stroke.

Historical abuses have created a legacy of mistrust that further complicates healthcare access. The Tuskegee Syphilis Study, in which Black men were deliberately left untreated for syphilis without their knowledge, and the unauthorized use of Henrietta Lacks' cells for research represent just two examples of medical exploitation that have left lasting scars. This historical context contributes to lower rates of participation in preventive care, clinical trials, and organ donation among communities of color.

Addressing racism in healthcare requires multilevel interventions: increasing diversity in healthcare professions, implementing anti-bias training for providers, improving cultural competence in medical education, expanding insurance coverage, investing in healthcare facilities in underserved communities, and addressing the social determinants of health that create unequal conditions. While healthcare disparities are partially a reflection of broader societal inequalities, the healthcare system itself must also confront and remediate the specific ways in which it perpetuates racial inequality in health outcomes.

Criminal Justice System Bias

The American criminal justice system exhibits some of the most stark and consequential racial disparities in our society. From initial encounters with police through sentencing and incarceration, people of color—particularly Black and Latino individuals—face systematically different treatment that cannot be explained by differences in crime rates alone. These disparities reflect and reinforce broader patterns of racial inequality while causing profound harm to individuals, families, and communities.

Racial disparities begin with policing practices. Research consistently shows that Black and Latino people are more likely to be stopped, searched, and arrested than white people, even when controlling for neighborhood characteristics and crime rates. Studies of traffic stops reveal that Black drivers are approximately 20% more likely to be stopped than white drivers and, once stopped, are searched at twice the rate, despite contraband being found less often. Stop-and-frisk programs have targeted people of color at dramatically disproportionate rates—in New York City's program, 87% of those stopped were Black or Latino, though these groups represented just over half the city's population.

These disparities continue through the adjudication process. Black and Latino defendants are more likely to be denied bail, offered less favorable plea deals, and sentenced more harshly than similarly situated white defendants. A comprehensive study by the U.S. Sentencing Commission found that Black male offenders received federal sentences that were 19.1% longer than those of similarly situated white male offenders. This disparity exists even when controlling for factors like criminal history, education, age, and weapon possession.

Arrest Disparities

Black Americans are arrested at 2.6 times the rate of white Americans, according to FBI data. For drug arrests specifically, Black people are 3.73 times more likely to be arrested for marijuana possession than white people, despite similar usage rates.

Pretrial Detention

Black and Latino defendants are more likely to be detained before trial due to inability to pay bail. This pretrial detention increases the likelihood of conviction and longer sentences, as detained defendants face more pressure to accept plea deals.

Use of Force

Data shows that police use force against Black people at significantly higher rates than against white people. Black Americans are 2.5 times more likely to be killed by police than white Americans, with unarmed Black individuals being particularly vulnerable.

The cumulative effect of these disparities is evident in incarceration statistics. Black Americans are incarcerated in state prisons at nearly five times the rate of white Americans, while Hispanic Americans are incarcerated at 1.3 times the rate. In some states, this disparity exceeds 10:1. As of 2020, Black Americans represented 38.3% of the federal prison population despite constituting only 13.4% of the U.S. population.

These disparities cannot be explained solely by differences in crime rates. While socioeconomic factors contribute to differential involvement in certain crimes, studies controlling for these factors still find significant racial disparities in justice system outcomes. Rather, these disparities reflect the culmination of discriminatory practices at each stage of the criminal justice process, from laws that disproportionately criminalize behaviors more common in communities of color (like crack versus powder cocaine penalties) to biased implementation of discretionary decisions by police, prosecutors, judges, and parole boards.

Policing and Mass Incarceration

The twin phenomena of aggressive policing and mass incarceration represent perhaps the most visible manifestations of systemic racism in contemporary America. Since the 1970s, the United States has embarked on an unprecedented expansion of its carceral system, with profoundly unequal impacts across racial lines. This system has devastated communities of color while failing to deliver proportionate public safety benefits.

The scale of American incarceration is truly exceptional in global context. With approximately 2 million people behind bars, the United States incarcerates more people than any other nation, both in absolute numbers and per capita. This mass incarceration emerged primarily from policy choices rather than crime rates, as incarceration continued to rise even during periods when crime was falling. These policy choices included mandatory minimum sentences, three-strikes laws, truth-in-sentencing requirements, and the War on Drugs, all of which disproportionately impacted communities of color.

Racial disparities permeate every aspect of this system. Black Americans are incarcerated at more than five times the rate of whites nationally, with even larger disparities in some states. One in three Black men born in 2001 can expect to be incarcerated during their lifetime, compared to one in seventeen white men. The War on Drugs has been particularly consequential in creating these disparities, with Black people representing approximately 33% of drug arrests despite making up only about 13% of drug users.

Aggressive policing tactics have often targeted communities of color explicitly. Stop-and-frisk programs in cities like New York disproportionately targeted Black and Latino residents, with over 85% of stops involving people of color. These programs subjected hundreds of thousands of innocent people to humiliating public searches while yielding minimal public safety benefits. Similarly, "broken windows" policing that focuses on minor infractions has led to excessive criminalization in low-income communities of color.

The consequences of mass incarceration extend far beyond prison walls. Approximately 77 million Americans have criminal records that create barriers to employment, housing, education, and public benefits. These collateral consequences disproportionately affect communities of color, creating cycles of disadvantage that span generations. Neighborhoods with high incarceration rates experience disrupted family structures, economic disinvestment, political disenfranchisement, and trauma that undermine community stability.

Recognizing these harms, reform movements have gained momentum in recent years. Initiatives include sentencing reforms, decriminalization of certain offenses, alternatives to incarceration, bail reform, and police accountability measures. However, meaningful transformation requires addressing not just specific policies but the underlying assumptions that have produced a system that monitors, controls, and incarcerates Black and brown people at such disproportionate rates. True reform must reckon with how profoundly race has shaped American approaches to crime, punishment, and public safety.

Voting Rights and Representation

The right to vote, which is fundamental to democratic participation, has been systematically denied or diluted for racial minorities throughout American history. From explicit disenfranchisement to more subtle contemporary barriers, voting rights remain a critical battleground in the struggle against systemic racism, with profound implications for political representation and policy outcomes.

The history of voting rights in America reveals a pattern of exclusion and resistance to inclusion of non-white voters. Following the brief period of Black enfranchisement during Reconstruction, Southern states implemented a comprehensive system of disenfranchisement through poll taxes, literacy tests, grandfather clauses, and violent intimidation. These measures reduced Black voter registration in some states to less than 5% by the early 20th century. Native Americans were denied U.S. citizenship until 1924, while citizenship restrictions effectively barred many Asian immigrants from voting until the mid-20th century.

The Voting Rights Act of 1965 marked a watershed moment, prohibiting discriminatory voting practices and establishing federal oversight of election procedures in states with histories of discrimination. This legislation produced dramatic increases in voter registration and the election of Black officials across the South. However, the Supreme Court's 2013 decision in *Shelby County v. Holder* struck down key provisions of the Voting Rights Act, eliminating the requirement that jurisdictions with histories of discrimination obtain federal preclearance before changing voting procedures.

Historical Voter Suppression Tactics

- Poll taxes requiring payment to vote
- Literacy tests applied unequally to different races
- White primaries excluding Black voters from meaningful elections
- Grandfather clauses exempting whites from voting restrictions
- Violence and intimidation against potential voters

Contemporary Barriers to Voting

- Strict voter ID requirements that disproportionately impact minorities
- Purges of voter rolls affecting eligible voters
- Reduced early voting opportunities in minority communities
- Polling place closures in predominantly minority areas
- Felony disenfranchisement affecting millions of Americans

Consequences for Representation

- Underrepresentation in elected offices at all levels
- Dilution of voting power through gerrymandering
- Policies that neglect the needs of underrepresented communities
- Decreased accountability to minority constituents
- Reinforcement of political inequality

In the wake of *Shelby County*, many states implemented new voting restrictions. These include strict voter ID laws, reductions in early voting opportunities, limitations on mail-in voting, and aggressive purging of voter rolls. While these measures are often justified as preventing fraud, evidence of widespread voter fraud is minimal, while research indicates these restrictions disproportionately burden voters of color. For example, studies have found that Black and Latino voters are less likely to possess the forms of ID required by strict ID laws and more likely to rely on early voting opportunities that have been curtailed.

Beyond direct barriers to voting, representational disparities persist through mechanisms like gerrymandering—the practice of drawing electoral districts to disadvantage certain groups. Courts have found numerous instances where states drew district lines specifically to dilute minority voting power. Additionally, the winner-take-all system used in most American elections tends to underrepresent minorities, while felony disenfranchisement laws in many states bar millions of citizens—disproportionately Black and Latino—from voting even after completing their sentences.

These barriers to equal voting rights have concrete consequences for representation and policy. Despite recent progress, racial minorities remain significantly underrepresented at all levels of government relative to their share of the population. This representational inequality translates into policies that often fail to address the needs of communities of color, perpetuating cycles of disadvantage. Ensuring equal access to the ballot thus remains essential to addressing systemic racism across all domains of American life.

Embedded Racism in Law and Government

The American legal system and government structures have historically been instrumental in creating and maintaining racial hierarchies. From the nation's founding through the present day, laws and policies have often served to exclude, control, and disadvantage racial minorities while protecting the privileges of the dominant group.

Early American law explicitly codified racial inequality, beginning with laws establishing chattel slavery and later expanding to restrict the rights of free Black people. The U.S. Constitution itself contained provisions that protected slavery, including the Three-Fifths Compromise and the Fugitive Slave Clause. After the Civil War, the brief period of progressive Reconstruction legislation was quickly undermined by Supreme Court decisions that severely limited federal protection of civil rights.

The legal framework of Jim Crow segregation that followed was comprehensive, separating races in public accommodations, transportation, schools, and even cemeteries across the South. The Supreme Court's decision in Plessy v. Ferguson (1896) enshrined the doctrine of "separate but equal," providing constitutional justification for legalized segregation that would stand for nearly 60 years. During this period, voting rights for Black Americans were systematically undermined through poll taxes, literacy tests, and other mechanisms explicitly designed to circumvent the 15th Amendment.

Property laws and government housing policies created and reinforced residential segregation throughout the 20th century. The Federal Housing Administration, established in 1934, institutionalized redlining through its underwriting manual, explicitly discouraging loans in areas with "inharmonious racial groups" and steering government-backed mortgages to white-only neighborhoods. These policies created lasting patterns of segregation and wealth inequality that persist today.

Exclusionary Citizenship

The Naturalization Act of 1790 limited naturalized citizenship to "free white persons." This racial restriction wasn't fully removed until 1952, meaning most non-white immigrants were ineligible for citizenship for most of American history.

Immigration Restrictions

Laws like the Chinese Exclusion Act of 1882 and the Immigration Act of 1924 established quotas and outright bans targeting specific racial and ethnic groups, fundamentally shaping the demographic composition of the United States.

Criminal Justice Disparities

From the Black Codes of the Reconstruction era to the disparate sentencing guidelines for crack versus powder cocaine in the 1980s, criminal laws have frequently been designed or implemented in ways that disproportionately target communities of color.

Even after landmark civil rights legislation of the 1960s prohibited explicit discrimination, the Supreme Court has often interpreted these protections narrowly. Recent decisions have weakened voting rights protections, limited affirmative action, restricted the scope of discrimination claims, and made it more difficult to challenge policies with disparate racial impacts.

Understanding how racism has been embedded in law and government is essential because these institutions establish the rules and frameworks that structure all other aspects of society. While explicitly discriminatory laws have largely been eliminated, their legacies continue to shape contemporary outcomes, and more subtle forms of legal discrimination persist in the criminal justice system, voting rights, and other domains.

The Role of Policy in Perpetuating Racism

Public policy serves as one of the most powerful mechanisms through which systemic racism operates and perpetuates across generations. Policies—whether federal, state, or local—establish the rules that govern resource allocation, determine access to opportunities, and shape the lived experiences of different racial groups. Even policies that appear race-neutral on their face can produce and maintain racial disparities when implemented within existing structures of inequality.

Historically, many American policies were explicitly designed to create racial hierarchies. Slave codes, Black codes, and Jim Crow laws directly codified racial inequality. Immigration policies like the Chinese Exclusion Act of 1882 and the nationality quotas of the Immigration Act of 1924 explicitly targeted specific racial and ethnic groups for exclusion. These overtly discriminatory policies laid the groundwork for contemporary disparities by establishing patterns of advantage and disadvantage that would persist long after the policies themselves were repealed.

In the post-Civil Rights era, policies have perpetuated racial inequality in more subtle ways. The "War on Drugs" initiated in the 1970s, for instance, was presented as race-neutral but resulted in dramatically higher incarceration rates for Black and Latino Americans, despite similar rates of drug use across racial groups. Mandatory minimum sentencing, three-strikes laws, and disparate penalties for crack versus powder cocaine all contributed to a system of mass incarceration with profound racial disparities.

Education funding policies that rely heavily on local property taxes perpetuate inequality by ensuring that schools in wealthy areas (which tend to be predominantly white due to historical housing discrimination) receive more resources than schools in lower-income areas (which tend to be more diverse). Transportation policies that prioritize highways serving suburban commuters over public transit in urban centers disproportionately benefit white communities while imposing environmental and economic costs on communities of color.

Environmental regulations with weak enforcement in low-income areas and communities of color have resulted in these communities bearing a disproportionate burden of pollution and environmental hazards. Meanwhile, tax policies that favor wealth over income provide greater benefits to white Americans, who hold significantly more wealth than Black or Latino Americans due to historical advantages in property ownership and inheritance.

Military Service

The intersection of war and racism in American history reveals how military conflict has both reinforced and occasionally disrupted racial hierarchies. From the Revolutionary War to contemporary conflicts, military service has been a contradictory space where racial oppression persists alongside opportunities for advancement and recognition.

Segregated Service

Throughout most of American history, military service has been segregated, with Black, Latino, Native American, and Asian American soldiers serving in separate units with limited opportunities for advancement. The "Double V" campaign during World War II highlighted the hypocrisy of fighting fascism abroad while maintaining racial segregation at home.

Conditional Citizenship

Military service has functioned as a conditional pathway to citizenship and civil rights for marginalized groups. The service of Black soldiers in the Civil War and both World Wars strengthened demands for equal rights, while Japanese American soldiers in the 442nd Regiment served with distinction even as their families remained in internment camps.

Racialized Enemies

American war propaganda has consistently dehumanized enemies through racial stereotypes, from anti-Japanese imagery during World War II to anti-Arab sentiment during conflicts in the Middle East. These racialized portrayals reinforce domestic racism against corresponding ethnic groups.

Unequal Burdens and Opportunities

The economic draft—where limited economic opportunities push marginalized communities toward military service—creates disproportionate exposure to combat risks. Communities of color have historically borne heavier casualties while receiving fewer benefits from their service. Despite comprising only 12.4% of the population, Black Americans represented 23% of Vietnam War casualties and continue to be overrepresented in front-line combat positions.

The GI Bill, which transformed post-WWII America by providing education and housing benefits to veterans, was administered in ways that largely excluded Black veterans. While white veterans used these benefits to access higher education and subsidized mortgages in growing suburbs, discriminatory implementation by local officials often denied the same opportunities to veterans of color, widening rather than narrowing the racial wealth gap.

Contemporary Military Racism

The modern volunteer military reflects ongoing tensions between inclusion and discrimination. While the military has formally integrated and implemented diversity initiatives, service members of color continue to report higher rates of harassment, receive disproportionate disciplinary actions, and face barriers to promotion into leadership positions. Muslim and Arab American service members have faced particular challenges in the post-9/11 era, often navigating suspicion and discrimination even while serving.

Veterans of color face compounded challenges when returning to civilian life, including higher rates of homelessness, employment discrimination, and difficulties accessing VA benefits. The toxic exposure from burn pits, Agent Orange, and other environmental hazards disproportionately impacts communities already facing environmental racism and healthcare disparities.

Anti-War Movements and Racial Justice

Historically, anti-war movements have sometimes forged powerful connections with racial justice struggles. Martin Luther King Jr.'s opposition to the Vietnam War linked the fight against racism at home with opposition to imperial violence abroad. Contemporary peace movements continue to highlight how militarism diverts resources from domestic needs while reinforcing systems of oppression. Indigenous activists have particularly emphasized connections between territorial conquest, resource extraction, and military expansion.

Movements for demilitarization of police departments draw explicit connections between domestic law enforcement and foreign military operations, noting the transfer of equipment, tactics, and surveillance technologies from war zones to urban communities of color. This "boomerang effect" of imperial violence returning home illustrates how systems of racism operate across domestic and international boundaries.

Foreign Policy

US foreign policy has been fundamentally shaped by racial hierarchies since the nation's founding, with systemic racism manifesting in both historical and contemporary approaches to international relations. The ideology of American exceptionalism has often been infused with notions of racial superiority, justifying interventionist policies in countries primarily populated by people of color.

US immigration policies have historically favored European immigrants while restricting entry from Asia, Africa, and Latin America. From the Chinese Exclusion Act to the "Muslim Ban," these policies reflect how racial hierarchies shape not only domestic but international relations.

Economic Relations and Development

International trade agreements and development aid often reproduce colonial power dynamics, with terms heavily favoring US interests while undermining economic sovereignty in Global South nations. World Bank and IMF structural adjustment programs have disproportionately impacted nations with majority non-white populations, enforcing austerity measures rarely demanded of European allies.

Military Intervention and Racial Dynamics

The threshold for military intervention appears significantly lower when target populations are predominantly non-white. The disproportionate civilian casualties in conflicts from Vietnam to Iraq to drone warfare in Africa and the Middle East reflect a devaluation of non-white lives in strategic calculations.

The persistence of these policy-driven disparities illustrates how systemic racism operates independently of individual intentions. Many policymakers may genuinely believe they are creating race-neutral policies, but without explicit consideration of how these policies interact with existing racial inequalities, they often end up reinforcing rather than remedying disparities. Understanding this dynamic is essential for developing policies that actively promote racial equity rather than passively perpetuating inequality.

Domestic Terrorism

Domestic terrorism in the United States has a long and troubling history deeply intertwined with systemic racism. The FBI defines domestic terrorism as violent acts committed by individuals or groups based in the US to further ideological goals stemming from domestic influences, such as political, religious, social, racial, or environmental beliefs.

Historical Context

From Reconstruction-era violence by the Ku Klux Klan to church bombings during the Civil Rights Movement, racially motivated domestic terrorism has been used as a tool to maintain racial hierarchy and suppress efforts toward equality.

Current Trends

According to government data, white supremacist extremism represents the most persistent and lethal domestic terrorism threat in contemporary America, with hate crimes and acts of domestic terrorism disproportionately targeting communities of color.

Systemic Implications

Beyond physical violence, the threat of domestic terrorism creates psychological trauma and restricts freedom of movement and expression for targeted groups, reinforcing systemic disadvantages and racial subjugation.

Racial Motivations and White Nationalism

Law enforcement agencies have identified racially motivated violent extremism, particularly white supremacist extremism, as the primary domestic terrorism threat in the United States today. Historical examples include the 1921 Tulsa Race Massacre, the 1963 16th Street Baptist Church bombing in Birmingham, and more recent attacks like the 2015 Charleston church shooting and the 2019 El Paso shooting targeting Latinos.

These acts of violence serve a dual purpose within the framework of systemic racism: they inflict immediate harm on communities of color while simultaneously sending a broader message meant to intimidate, control, and maintain racial power structures. The connection between hate groups, domestic terrorism, and mainstream institutions has often been minimized in official narratives, reflecting a reluctance to confront the depth of racial animus in American society.

Unequal Response and Enforcement

The government's response to domestic terrorism has historically reflected racial disparities embedded in the larger criminal justice system. Terrorism by white supremacist groups has frequently received less aggressive investigation and prosecution compared to other forms of extremism. This inconsistent application of counterterrorism resources represents another manifestation of systemic racism, where threats to communities of color are accorded lower priority.

Additionally, counterterrorism policies have sometimes disproportionately targeted Muslim, Arab, and South Asian American communities, particularly after September 11, 2001, reflecting how racial and religious profiling can be institutionalized within national security frameworks.

Community Impact and Resilience

For communities of color, domestic terrorism creates layers of trauma beyond the immediate violence. Places of worship, cultural centers, and other community gathering spaces become sites of both vulnerability and resilience. The psychological impact of living under threat of racial violence contributes to racial stress and trauma that compound other effects of systemic racism.

Despite these challenges, targeted communities have developed response strategies, security networks, and healing practices that represent important forms of resistance to terror-enforced racial hierarchies. These community-based approaches often address needs that official security responses fail to recognize or prioritize.

Employment and Workplace Discrimination

Despite decades of civil rights legislation, racial discrimination persists in American workplaces, creating barriers to economic opportunity and mobility for people of color. From hiring and promotion to workplace culture and compensation, racial disparities in employment contribute significantly to broader patterns of economic inequality along racial lines.

Unemployment rates consistently reveal racial disparities that cannot be explained by education or other factors. Even before the COVID-19 pandemic, the unemployment rate for Black Americans typically ran about twice that of white Americans, with Hispanic unemployment also consistently higher than white unemployment. These gaps persist across education levels: Black college graduates face unemployment rates similar to those of white Americans with some college but no degree. During economic downturns, workers of color typically experience earlier job losses and slower recovery, a pattern clearly demonstrated during both the 2008 recession and the COVID-19 pandemic.

Experimental studies have repeatedly demonstrated discrimination in hiring processes. Resume audit studies, in which identical resumes are submitted with only the names changed to suggest different racial identities, consistently show that resumes with "white-sounding" names receive 50% more callbacks than identical resumes with "Black-sounding" names. Similar discrimination has been documented against applicants with Hispanic, Asian, and Middle Eastern names. This discrimination occurs across industries and job types, affecting even highly educated professionals.

For those who secure employment, workplace experiences often differ substantially by race. People of color report higher rates of harassment, microaggressions, and hostile work environments. Studies document that Black and Latino employees receive more scrutiny and criticism than their white counterparts performing identical work. These negative experiences contribute to higher stress levels, reduced job satisfaction, and higher turnover rates among employees of color.

Promotional opportunities and wage growth also show racial disparities. People of color are underrepresented in management and leadership positions across industries—a phenomenon often referred to as the "glass ceiling" for minorities. According to federal data, while people of color constitute approximately 40% of the U.S. population, they hold only 17% of executive-level positions in the private sector. This underrepresentation in leadership limits career advancement for employees of color while perpetuating workplace cultures that may be less inclusive.

Wage gaps persist even when controlling for education, experience, and occupation. Black men earn approximately 70 cents and Hispanic men earn about 69 cents for every dollar earned by white men in similar positions. The gaps are even larger for women of color, with Black women earning 61 cents and Hispanic women earning 53 cents compared to white men, reflecting the intersection of racial and gender discrimination.

Addressing workplace discrimination requires comprehensive approaches, including stronger enforcement of anti-discrimination laws, anonymous hiring practices, mentorship programs, diversity initiatives with accountability measures, and addressing unconscious bias in evaluations and promotions. As one of the primary mechanisms for economic mobility, equal opportunity in employment is essential to dismantling systemic racism more broadly.

Economic Opportunity and Inequality

Racial disparities in economic opportunity represent one of the most persistent and consequential manifestations of systemic racism in the United States. These disparities extend across multiple dimensions—from income and wealth to entrepreneurship and economic mobility—creating structural barriers that limit the economic potential of communities of color while preserving advantages for white Americans.

Income inequality along racial lines remains stubbornly entrenched in the American economy. According to Census Bureau data, in 2019 (before the pandemic's economic disruptions), the median household income was $76,057 for white households, $56,113 for Hispanic households, and $45,438 for Black households. These disparities persist even when controlling for education levels. Black workers with bachelor's degrees earn approximately 20% less than similarly educated white workers, and this gap has actually widened since 1980.

The racial wealth gap is even more pronounced than income disparities. While income represents current earnings, wealth—the total value of a family's assets minus debts—provides economic security, enables investments in education and entrepreneurship, and can be transferred across generations. According to Federal Reserve data, the median white family has about eight times the wealth of the median Black family and five times the wealth of the median Hispanic family. This wealth gap has roots in historical policies like slavery, segregation, and redlining, but continues to be reinforced by contemporary systems.

Entrepreneurship and business ownership show similar patterns of disparity. While approximately 13% of the U.S. population is Black, Black-owned businesses account for only about 2% of all U.S. businesses with employees. Hispanic-owned businesses represent about 6% of employer businesses despite Hispanics constituting about 18% of the population. These businesses face systematic barriers to formation, growth, and sustainability, including reduced access to capital, smaller professional networks, and discrimination from potential customers, suppliers, and lenders.

Economic mobility—the ability to improve one's economic position over time or across generations—is also stratified by race. Research by economist Raj Chetty and colleagues found that Black Americans experience lower rates of upward mobility and higher rates of downward mobility than white Americans across all income levels. Even Black children born to parents in the top income quintile are more likely to fall to the bottom quintile as adults than to remain at the top, a pattern of downward mobility rarely seen among white Americans.

These economic disparities reflect the cumulative impact of historical exclusion and ongoing discrimination across multiple systems. Labor market discrimination limits employment opportunities and earnings. Educational inequities restrict skill development and credentials.

Housing segregation affects access to jobs, services, and amenities. Banking discrimination constrains access to capital. Each of these mechanisms reinforces the others, creating durable patterns of economic disadvantage that persist despite individual efforts at advancement.

Addressing economic inequality requires interventions at multiple levels, from strengthening anti-discrimination laws and enforcement to targeted investments in historically disadvantaged communities. Programs that build assets and create pathways to business ownership can help address the wealth gap, while improvements in education and workforce development can enhance earning potential. However, meaningful progress requires recognizing that current disparities are not simply the result of individual choices but rather reflect systemic barriers that must be dismantled through deliberate policy action.

Business and Entrepreneurship

The American business landscape reflects and reinforces the country's racial hierarchies through systematic barriers that limit entrepreneurial opportunities for people of color. Historical exclusion from business ownership, combined with contemporary obstacles, has created persistent disparities in who can successfully start, sustain, and grow businesses in the United States.

Financing

Black and Latino entrepreneurs face significant barriers when seeking access to capital, with studies consistently showing loan denial rates for minority business enterprises

(MBEs) at nearly three times the rate of white-owned businesses with comparable credit profiles. When approved, MBEs typically receive smaller amounts at higher interest rates, creating immediate disadvantages in market competition.

Wealth Gap and Startup Resources

The racial wealth gap directly impacts entrepreneurship, as most startups initially rely on personal savings and family resources. With the median white family possessing approximately ten times the wealth of the median Black family, entrepreneurs of color have significantly less cushion for initial investments, market downturns, or expansion opportunities.

Network Exclusion

Social capital and professional networks remain largely segregated, limiting access to mentorship, investor relationships, and business opportunities for entrepreneurs of color. Industry connections that facilitate introductions to key decision-makers, strategic partnerships, and market insights disproportionately benefit white entrepreneurs through existing networks of privilege.

Structural Barriers in Business Development

Beyond startup challenges, systemic barriers continue throughout the business lifecycle. Procurement policies, supplier diversity initiatives, and government contracting often maintain racial disparities despite nominal inclusion efforts. Studies show that less than 2% of government contracts go to Black-owned businesses, while corporate supplier diversity programs frequently fail to move beyond symbolic gestures.

The venture capital landscape exhibits particularly stark disparities, with Black founders receiving less than 1% of all venture funding despite representing over 13% of the U.S. population. Latino founders fare similarly, receiving approximately 2% of venture investments. These funding gaps directly impact innovation opportunities, market growth, and wealth creation potential for communities of color.

Regulatory and Market Discrimination

Licensing requirements, zoning regulations, and other market governance structures often disproportionately burden minority entrepreneurs. Research demonstrates that industries with heavy licensure requirements show lower rates of minority ownership, while neighborhood-based businesses in communities of color face additional hurdles including higher insurance rates, security costs, and customer base limitations resulting from residential segregation patterns.

Banking relationships remain fraught with discriminatory practices, from branch location decisions that create "banking deserts" in communities of color to relationship banking models that disadvantage newcomers to financial systems. The Community Reinvestment Act has proven insufficient to address these systematic deficiencies in financial service provision.

Resistance and Alternative Models

Despite these barriers, entrepreneurs of color have created innovative responses, including the development of community-based financial institutions, cooperative business models, and advocacy organizations focused on economic justice. These efforts have established important alternatives to traditional business frameworks while simultaneously challenging the existing system's inequities.

Recent movements toward supporting Black-owned businesses, impact investing in disadvantaged communities, and addressing supplier diversity have shown promise, though structural reforms addressing underlying wealth disparities, discriminatory lending, and segregated networks remain essential for meaningful change in America's entrepreneurial landscape.

Access to Capital and Banking

The financial system plays a crucial role in economic opportunity, yet communities of color face persistent barriers in accessing banking services, loans, and investment capital. These disparities in financial access represent a significant dimension of systemic racism, limiting wealth-building opportunities and economic development in minority communities.

Banking access remains unequal along racial lines. According to FDIC data, approximately 13.8% of Black households and 12.2% of Hispanic households are unbanked (lacking any bank account), compared to just 2.5% of white households. Additionally, 24.9% of Black households and 21.7% of Hispanic households are underbanked (having an account but relying on alternative financial services like check cashing services or payday loans), compared to 10.3% of white households. This limited access to mainstream banking forces many families to rely on costly alternative financial services that extract wealth from communities already facing economic challenges.

Geographic distribution of banking services contributes to these disparities. Bank branch closures have disproportionately affected low-income and minority neighborhoods, creating "banking deserts" where residents must travel significant distances to access services. Meanwhile, high-cost alternative financial services like check cashers and payday lenders concentrate in these same communities, creating a two-tier financial system divided largely along racial lines.

Loan Application

Minority applicants face higher rejection rates even with identical financial profiles as white applicants

Interest Rates

Approved minority borrowers often receive higher interest rates and less favorable terms

Loan Amounts

Minority borrowers typically receive smaller loan amounts relative to their needs and qualifications

Banking Relationship

Minority customers report less supportive relationships with financial institutions

Discriminatory lending practices constitute perhaps the most significant barrier to capital access. Studies consistently document racial disparities in mortgage lending, with Black and Hispanic applicants approximately twice as likely to be denied conventional mortgages as white applicants with similar financial characteristics. When minorities do receive loans, they often pay higher interest rates and fees. A 2020 study found that Black borrowers pay approximately $13,464 more over the life of a home loan than similarly situated white borrowers, effectively imposing a "racism tax" on homeownership.

Small business financing shows similar patterns of disparity. According to Federal Reserve data, Black-owned businesses are approximately twice as likely to be denied loans as white-owned businesses, even when controlling for factors like credit scores and business performance. When approved, minority-owned businesses typically receive smaller loan amounts and less favorable terms. During the COVID-19 pandemic, these disparities became particularly visible in the distribution of Paycheck Protection Program loans, with businesses in majority-white neighborhoods receiving loans more quickly and in larger amounts than those in majority-Black areas.

Beyond traditional lending, venture capital and investment funding flow disproportionately to white entrepreneurs. Black founders received just 1.2% of the $147 billion in venture capital invested in U.S. startups in 2021, while Latino founders received approximately 2%. This limited access to growth capital restricts the scale and impact of minority-owned businesses, constraining job creation and wealth building in communities of color.

Addressing these disparities requires comprehensive approaches: strengthening fair lending laws and enforcement, expanding community banking and credit union presence in underserved areas, developing alternative credit scoring models that don't perpetuate historical disadvantage, supporting minority-owned financial institutions, and creating targeted capital access programs for underserved communities. Equal access to financial services and capital is essential not just for individual economic opportunity but for building community wealth and addressing the racial wealth gap.

Media and Cultural Representation

Media and cultural representations powerfully shape how we understand race and racial differences. From news coverage to entertainment media to advertising, representations of racial and ethnic groups influence public perceptions, reinforce or challenge stereotypes, and help determine which voices and perspectives are centered in public discourse. Systemic racism operates through these representations, often in ways that naturalize racial hierarchies while appearing neutral or objective.

News media plays a particularly significant role in shaping understandings of race, especially around issues of crime, poverty, and social problems. Research consistently documents patterns of racialized coverage that associate crime more strongly with Black and Latino Americans than with whites. A 2020 analysis of local TV news found that Black Americans were overrepresented as criminal suspects relative to actual crime statistics, while being underrepresented as victims. Similarly, poverty is often visually represented through images of Black and Latino Americans, even though the majority of poor Americans are white, contributing to racialized understandings of economic disadvantage.

Entertainment media has historically promoted harmful stereotypes while limiting complex representations of people of color. From early depictions of Black Americans as subservient or threatening, to portrayals of Latinos as exotic or criminal, to representations of Asian Americans as perpetual foreigners or "model minorities," these stereotypical characters have shaped public perceptions in lasting ways. While representation has improved in recent decades, studies still document significant underrepresentation of racial minorities in leading roles, complex characters, and behind-the-camera positions where creative decisions are made.

The lack of diversity in media leadership positions remains particularly problematic. According to the Columbia Journalism Review, people of color made up just 22.6% of television news directors and 13.5% of newspaper editors as of 2020, despite constituting nearly 40% of the U.S. population. In Hollywood, minorities held just 12.6% of writing positions and 7.8% of directing jobs for top-grossing films. This underrepresentation in decision-making roles affects which stories are told, whose perspectives are centered, and how racial issues are framed and contextualized.

Social media has created new opportunities for diverse voices but has also enabled the rapid spread of racist content and misinformation. Algorithms that prioritize engagement often amplify extremist content, while platform policies inconsistently moderate racist language and imagery. Studies have documented how facial recognition technologies and image-generation algorithms reflect and reinforce racial biases, suggesting that emerging technologies may reproduce rather than disrupt patterns of discriminatory representation.

Advertising and marketing materials similarly reflect and reinforce racial stereotypes, from the association of certain products with particular racial groups to the limited representation of people of color in luxury goods marketing. Even when minority representation increases, it often takes the form of "tokenism" that includes racial diversity without meaningfully challenging stereotypes or centering diverse perspectives.

More equitable media representation requires structural changes: diversifying leadership and creative positions, developing more nuanced storytelling that avoids stereotypes, implementing content analysis to identify patterns of bias, and supporting media created by and for communities of color. As one of the primary means through which Americans form understandings of racial difference, media reform represents an essential component of addressing systemic racism.

Music Industry

The American music industry represents one of the most visible arenas where racial exploitation, cultural appropriation, and systemic barriers have operated alongside creative resistance and cultural innovation. From its earliest commercial development, the industry has reflected and reinforced broader patterns of racial inequality while simultaneously providing spaces for counternarratives and resistance.

Historical Exploitation

Black musicians were routinely denied royalties, forced to sign exploitative contracts, and watched as white artists covered their songs for greater profit. Record companies maintained segregated "race records" divisions that paid Black artists a fraction of what white artists earned for similar commercial success.

Appropriation of Genres

From jazz and blues to rock and roll, hip-hop and R&B, genres pioneered by Black musicians have been historically repackaged and marketed through white performers who received greater industry support, radio play, and financial rewards.

Industry Gatekeeping

The power structures within record labels, radio stations, and industry awards have remained disproportionately white, creating systemic barriers for artists of color despite their cultural influence and creative contributions.

Historical Patterns of Exploitation

The commodification of Black musical innovation began in the early 20th century, when record companies systematically exploited Black blues and jazz musicians. Artists like Robert Johnson and Bessie Smith died in poverty despite creating foundational American music. The birth of rock and roll represents perhaps the most visible example of racial erasure, as Black pioneers like Sister Rosetta Tharpe, Little Richard, and Chuck Berry were pushed aside while white artists achieved greater fame performing their innovations.

"The way in which many white Americans have heard Black music has been the result of a series of distorting lenses that have been placed between them and the original sounds." - Nelson George, music historian

Industry Representation

Despite creating music that dominates charts across genres, artists of color continue to face discrimination in record deals, marketing budgets, and award recognition. A 2021 industry report revealed that only 19.8% of music executives at major labels were from underrepresented racial/ethnic groups, despite these communities driving much of modern music culture.

Digital Platforms and Algorithms

Streaming platforms and recommendation algorithms have been shown to reproduce existing biases, often directing listeners toward artists who match demographic profiles rather than musical styles. This digital redlining creates new barriers for artists of color to reach audiences beyond predetermined categories.

Genre Segregation

The industry continues to segregate artists into racialized genre categories that impact marketing, distribution, and award recognition. Black artists are often restricted to "urban" categories regardless of their musical style, while white artists adopting similar sounds are marketed in more lucrative "pop" categories.

Inequitable Contracts

Studies show persistent disparities in contract terms offered to artists of color compared to white counterparts, including lower advances, higher recoupment requirements, and more restrictive intellectual property terms, perpetuating wealth gaps among creators.

Resistance and Progress

Artists of color have consistently found ways to challenge the industry's racist structures. The rise of independent labels in the 1960s and 1970s created alternative pathways, while hip-hop's DIY ethos in the 1980s and 1990s established new business models. Digital technology has further enabled artists to bypass traditional gatekeepers, though major platforms and distributors still wield significant power.

Recent years have seen growing recognition of these issues, with major labels pledging to address inequities following the 2020 racial justice protests. However, critics note that substantive structural changes remain elusive, with temporary initiatives often substituting for deeper reform of business practices, leadership composition, and resource allocation.

The music industry continues to serve as both a reflection of America's racial hierarchies and a potential laboratory for more equitable models of cultural production and exchange. The struggle for racial justice in music remains inextricably linked to broader movements for economic, social, and cultural equity.

Advertising and Media Buying

Advertising and media buying represent critical components of the marketing ecosystem where systemic racism has been deeply embedded. Media buying—the process of purchasing advertising space and time across various platforms—has historically excluded and undervalued media outlets serving communities of color while concentrating economic power in predominantly white-owned agencies and networks.

Disparities in Media Investment

Despite the substantial buying power of Black, Hispanic, and Asian American communities (estimated at over $4.5 trillion combined), advertising spending targeted to these demographics remains disproportionately low. Black-focused media outlets receive less than 2% of total advertising dollars despite Black Americans representing 13.4% of the population.

Devaluation of Minority Markets

Research has revealed that advertisers routinely pay 35-70% less for ad placements targeting Black and Hispanic audiences compared to white audiences of similar size and demographics. This "ethnic discount" reflects and reinforces systemic devaluation of these communities as consumers.

Exclusionary Media Planning

Media planners frequently exclude Black, Hispanic, and Asian media outlets from advertising campaigns based on unfounded stereotypes about audience income levels, purchasing behaviors, or brand affinity. Many agencies maintain "no urban/no Hispanic" dictates that explicitly exclude these outlets without legitimate business justification.

Structural Barriers in the Industry

The advertising and media buying industry operates through complex networks of agencies, clients, and media platforms that frequently disadvantage minority-owned businesses and professionals. Major holding companies control approximately 80% of global advertising spend while maintaining workforces that remain predominantly white, especially in leadership positions.

Ownership Disparities

Less than 2% of advertising agencies are Black-owned, and these firms face systematic barriers including limited access to capital, exclusion from RFP processes, and requirements for prohibitively high minimum billings. When minority-owned agencies are included, they're frequently pigeonholed into "multicultural" specialties rather than competing for general market accounts.

Measurement and Data Bias

Industry-standard audience measurement systems have historically undercounted minority audiences, particularly in traditional media. Nielsen ratings and similar metrics frequently underrepresent Black, Hispanic, and Asian American viewership due to methodological limitations and sampling biases, creating artificial justifications for lower advertising rates.

Digital Advertising and Algorithmic Discrimination

The shift to programmatic and algorithmic ad buying has introduced new forms of technological discrimination. Multiple studies have documented how digital platforms enable and sometimes enhance discriminatory practices:

- Ad delivery algorithms frequently show different job and housing opportunities based on perceived user race, even when advertisers attempt to target broadly
- Content featuring people of color is more likely to be flagged as "brand unsafe" by contextual targeting systems
- Black creators on platforms like YouTube and TikTok report systematic demonetization of their content compared to similar content from white creators
- Keyword exclusion lists routinely block ads from appearing alongside content related to racial justice, effectively defunding discussions about racism

Reform Efforts and Industry Response

In response to mounting criticism and activism, various initiatives have emerged to address systemic racism in advertising and media buying:

- The "Diversity in Advertising" commitment signed by major brands pledging to increase spending with Black-owned media
- The AIMM (Alliance for Inclusive and Multicultural Marketing) Cultural Insights Impact Measure to quantify the impact of cultural relevance in advertising
- Group Black, Dentsu's Economic Empowerment offering, and similar initiatives designed to redirect advertising dollars to minority-owned media
- The 4A's Equity & Inclusion Congress working to address structural barriers within agencies

However, these efforts remain nascent, and critics note that similar initiatives in the past have failed to produce lasting change. Meaningful reform will require fundamental restructuring of how media value is assigned, how advertising budgets are allocated, and how agency-client relationships are formed and maintained.

The discriminatory patterns in advertising and media buying connect directly to broader systems of economic exclusion while simultaneously reinforcing cultural stereotypes and media representation issues discussed in previous sections. As both an economic and cultural force, advertising represents a critical domain where systemic racism continues to operate despite increased awareness and calls for change.

The Role of Religion and Faith Institutions

Religious Justifications for Racism

Throughout American history, religious doctrines and institutions have frequently provided moral justification for racial hierarchy. Christian interpretations of biblical passages like the "Curse of Ham" were used to legitimize slavery as divinely ordained. Religious leaders developed elaborate theological arguments claiming that racial segregation reflected God's intended order for humanity. These religious justifications allowed proponents of racial hierarchy to frame discrimination not merely as expedient but as morally righteous.

Some religious institutions actively participated in racist systems through their own discriminatory practices. Many white churches excluded Black members or relegated them to segregated seating. Religious schools and universities maintained racially exclusionary admissions policies well into the 20th century. Missionary activities often characterized non-Christian cultural practices as primitive or evil, contributing to cultural erasure and internalized racism among converts. These institutional practices reinforced racial hierarchy while providing spiritual sanction for broader societal discrimination.

Faith-Based Resistance to Racism

Simultaneously, religious institutions and theologies have provided crucial foundations for resistance to racism. The Black church tradition played a central role in the abolitionist movement and civil rights struggle, providing organizational infrastructure, leadership development, and theological framing that located racial justice work within sacred obligation. Religious concepts of human dignity, beloved community, and divine justice offered moral language for articulating demands for equality.

Interfaith coalitions have frequently mobilized around racial justice issues, using moral authority to challenge discriminatory policies and practices. The Southern Christian Leadership Conference under Martin Luther King Jr.'s direction explicitly framed civil rights activism as an expression of Christian ethics. Jewish leaders and institutions participated significantly in civil rights organizing, drawing on religious traditions emphasizing justice and liberation. These faith-based movements demonstrated the potential of religious resources to challenge rather than reinforce racial hierarchy.

Contemporary American religious landscapes continue to reflect racial division while also offering spaces for bridging racial differences. Sunday morning remains what Martin Luther King Jr. called "the most segregated hour in

America," with approximately 80% of congregations having at least 90% of members from a single racial group. This segregation results from both historical patterns and ongoing preferences for cultural familiarity in worship styles. However, multiracial congregations have grown in recent decades, increasing from 7.5% of congregations in 1998 to 16% in 2019. These communities potentially provide rare spaces for meaningful cross-racial relationship development in a society where residential and educational segregation limits such opportunities.

Religious approaches to racial reconciliation display significant variation in analysis and prescription. Conservative approaches often emphasize individual prejudice and interpersonal harmony while minimizing structural dimensions of racism. Progressive religious perspectives typically incorporate systemic analysis and connect racial justice work to broader social transformation. Indigenous religious traditions frequently emphasize healing historical trauma and reclaiming cultural practices suppressed through colonization. These diverse approaches reflect the complex role of religion in both maintaining and challenging racial hierarchy, demonstrating how faith institutions remain important sites for contesting the meaning and implications of race in American society.

The Impact of Institutional Racism in STEMM

Science, technology, engineering, mathematics, and medicine (STEMM) fields have long been presented as meritocratic domains where objective evaluation of evidence and talent should transcend racial bias. However, substantial evidence indicates that systemic racism operates within these fields just as in other institutions, creating barriers to entry and advancement for scientists and healthcare providers of color while shaping research priorities and medical practices in ways that disadvantage minority communities.

Representation in STEMM fields reveals persistent racial disparities. Despite constituting approximately 13% of the U.S. population, Black Americans represent only about 9% of STEMM bachelor's degree recipients, 7% of STEMM master's recipients, and just 4% of STEMM doctoral recipients. These disparities become more pronounced at higher levels of the academic hierarchy: Black and Hispanic scientists make up less than 5% of full professors in STEMM fields at U.S. universities. In medicine, only 5% of physicians identify as Black and 5.8% as Hispanic/Latino, creating significant gaps in culturally competent healthcare provision.

These representation gaps stem from multiple barriers along the educational and career pipeline. In K-12 education, schools serving predominantly minority students often have fewer resources for science education, including less access to advanced courses, laboratory facilities, and experienced science teachers. Bias in advising and mentoring can discourage students of color from pursuing STEMM majors, while stereotype threat—the fear of confirming negative stereotypes about one's group—can undermine academic performance in these fields.

Even after entering STEMM careers, professionals of color face additional barriers to advancement. Studies of scientific grant funding reveal significant disparities: a 2011 study found that Black applicants were 10 percentage points less likely than white applicants to receive National

Institutes of Health (NIH) research funding, even after controlling for educational background, previous research awards, and publication record. Similar disparities have been documented in publication acceptance rates, speaking invitations, and citation patterns, creating cumulative disadvantages for researchers of color.

Beyond career obstacles for individual scientists, systemic racism shapes the very content and priorities of scientific research and medical practice. Historical abuses like the Tuskegee Syphilis Study have created lasting mistrust, while underrepresentation of racial minorities in clinical trials continues to limit knowledge about treatment efficacy across populations. Research questions relevant to minority communities often receive less funding and attention, creating gaps in knowledge about conditions that disproportionately affect these populations.

In medicine, racial bias affects diagnosis and treatment decisions even among well-intentioned providers. Studies document that Black patients receive less pain medication than white patients with identical symptoms and conditions. Algorithmic tools used in healthcare settings have been found to incorporate racial biases that direct fewer resources to Black patients, even when they have the same level of need as white patients. Medical education often presents biological differences between racial groups in ways that can reinforce harmful stereotypes rather than improve care.

Addressing systemic racism in STEMM requires comprehensive approaches: expanding pathways into these fields through educational investments, reforming grant review and publication processes to reduce bias, increasing diversity in leadership positions, incorporating anti-racism training in STEMM education, and prioritizing research questions relevant to diverse communities. As fields that significantly influence health outcomes, technological development, and economic opportunity, STEMM disciplines must confront and address their role in perpetuating racial inequality.

Environmental Racism

Environmental racism refers to the disproportionate exposure of communities of color to environmental hazards and limited access to environmental benefits. This pattern of inequality reflects how racial discrimination shapes decisions about land use, infrastructure investment, industrial siting, and environmental enforcement, creating disparate health outcomes and quality of life for different racial groups.

The distribution of environmental hazards reveals stark racial disparities. Communities with higher percentages of racial minorities are significantly more likely to be located near polluting industrial facilities, toxic waste sites, landfills, and other locally unwanted land uses (LULUs). A 2021 study in the journal Environmental Science & Technology Letters found that most categories of air pollution disproportionately affect people of color, regardless of income level or geography. Black Americans are 75% more likely than white Americans to live in "fence-line" communities near commercial facilities that produce noise, odor, traffic, or emissions that directly affect the population.

These disparities emerge through multiple mechanisms. Historically, discriminatory zoning practices concentrated industrial facilities in or near communities of color, while restrictive covenants and redlining prevented residents from moving to cleaner neighborhoods. The lower property values in these areas—themselves a product of racism—create economic incentives for polluting industries to locate there. When communities attempt to resist new hazardous facilities, those with more resources, political connections, and access to legal expertise—disproportionately white communities—are more successful in keeping such facilities out, a phenomenon known as "NIMBY" (Not In My Back Yard).

Enforcement of environmental regulations also shows racial disparities. The EPA's Office of Civil Rights has historically failed to effectively address Title VI complaints alleging discriminatory impacts from environmental permitting decisions. A 2015 analysis found that when facilities violate environmental laws, penalties are lower in areas with more minority and low-income residents than in predominantly white areas for comparable violations. Clean-up of contaminated sites also proceeds more slowly in minority communities, prolonging exposure to harmful substances.

The consequences of these disparities are evident in health outcomes. Rates of asthma, lead poisoning, and certain cancers are higher in communities with greater environmental burdens, which are disproportionately communities of color. During extreme weather events, which are becoming more frequent due to climate change, these communities often have fewer resources for evacuation, temporary housing, and recovery, as dramatically demonstrated during Hurricane Katrina in 2005 and subsequent disasters.

Access to environmental benefits like parks, green spaces, tree canopy, and outdoor recreation opportunities is similarly unequal. A 2020 study found that neighborhoods that are predominantly non-white have, on average, 44% less tree canopy than predominantly white neighborhoods. This disparity affects not only quality of life but also physical health through reduced air quality and increased urban heat island effects, which can be deadly during heat waves.

Toxic Facility Siting

Race is the strongest predictor of proximity to hazardous waste facilities, even controlling for income, land values, and other non-racial factors

Water Infrastructure

Communities of color face higher rates of drinking water violations and aging infrastructure, as exemplified by the Flint water crisis

Green Space Access

Predominantly white neighborhoods have 44% more tree canopy coverage than predominantly non-white neighborhoods

Climate Vulnerability

Communities of color face higher risks from climate change impacts like extreme heat, flooding, and air pollution

The environmental justice movement emerged in response to these disparities, combining civil rights advocacy with environmental protection goals. This movement has achieved some successes in preventing new facilities in overburdened communities and securing clean-up of contaminated sites. However, addressing environmental racism comprehensively requires reforming permitting processes, strengthening enforcement in affected communities, investing in environmental benefits for historically disadvantaged areas, and ensuring that climate policies benefit rather than further burden communities of color.

Native American Experiences

Even though the discussion of systemic racism in America and in this book centers on the experiences of Black Americans, Native American communities face unique manifestations of systemic racism that differ in important ways. These distinctive patterns of discrimination and disadvantage are rooted in the colonial history of the United States and the legal status of tribal nations, creating complex challenges at the intersection of race, sovereignty, and historical trauma.

The foundation of systemic racism against Native Americans lies in the history of colonization, land dispossession, and cultural genocide. From the earliest European settlement through the 19th century, federal policies explicitly aimed to eliminate Native nations through warfare, forced relocation, and the breaking up of tribal lands. The 1830 Indian Removal Act forced eastern tribes to territories west of the Mississippi, resulting in thousands of deaths on what became known as the Trail of Tears. Later, the Dawes Act of 1887 divided communal tribal lands into individual allotments, resulting in the loss of approximately 90 million acres—nearly two-thirds of the tribal land base—by 1934.

Cultural genocide policies targeted Native American identities, languages, and family structures. From the 1870s through the 1970s, Native children were systematically removed from their families and placed in boarding schools designed to "Kill the Indian, Save the Man" through forced assimilation. Children were prohibited from speaking their languages or practicing their traditions, while experiencing high rates of physical and sexual abuse. Later, the Indian Adoption Project placed Native children with non-Native families, separating them from their communities and cultural heritage. These policies created intergenerational trauma that continues to affect Native communities today.

Contemporary manifestations of systemic racism against Native Americans include severe disparities across multiple domains. In education, Native students have the lowest high school graduation rates of any racial group at 74%, compared to the national average of 86%. Health disparities are equally stark: Native Americans have a life expectancy 5.5 years shorter than the overall U.S. population, with higher rates of diabetes, heart disease, liver disease, and suicide. The Indian Health Service, responsible for providing healthcare to many Native Americans, is chronically underfunded, receiving approximately 50% of estimated need.

Economic conditions on many reservations reflect historic and ongoing marginalization. According to Census data, Native Americans have the highest poverty rate of any racial group at 25.4%, nearly twice the national average. Unemployment on reservations often exceeds 40%, while infrastructure deficits are severe—14% of Native American households lack access to electricity, and approximately 30% lack access to broadband internet, limiting educational and economic opportunities.

The legal status of tribal nations creates unique jurisdictional challenges that compound these disparities. Criminal justice jurisdiction on tribal lands is divided between tribal, federal, and sometimes state authorities, creating gaps in law enforcement that contribute to high rates of crime, particularly against Native women. According to Department of Justice data, more than 84% of Native women experience violence in their lifetime, with murder rates more than ten times the national average in some areas. Limited tribal jurisdiction over non-Native offenders has created what some advocates describe as a "hunting ground" for those seeking to evade justice.

Environmental injustice affects many Native communities, with tribal lands disproportionately affected by resource extraction, toxic waste disposal, and infrastructure projects that threaten sacred sites and natural resources. The Dakota Access Pipeline protests at Standing Rock in 2016 highlighted these ongoing conflicts between tribal sovereignty, environmental protection, and economic development controlled by non-Native interests.

Addressing systemic racism against Native Americans requires approaches that recognize both racial discrimination and the unique legal status of tribal nations. This includes honoring treaty obligations, strengthening tribal sovereignty, increasing funding for essential services, protecting cultural and religious freedom, and addressing the legacy of historical trauma through truth and reconciliation processes. Unlike other forms of anti-racism work, these efforts must acknowledge that Native Americans are not simply minority groups seeking inclusion but sovereign nations with inherent rights to self-determination.

Latino and Immigrant Communities

Latino communities in the United States face distinctive patterns of systemic racism that are shaped by the intersection of racial identity, ethnicity, language, and immigration status. While the Latino population is extremely diverse—encompassing people with origins in over 20 countries, different racial identities, and varying immigration histories—certain common experiences of discrimination and disadvantage affect many members of these communities.

Immigration status creates a fundamental axis of vulnerability for many Latinos. Approximately 19% of Latinos in the U.S. are immigrants without legal status, making them vulnerable to exploitation in employment, housing, and other domains. Fear of deportation often prevents reporting of workplace violations, domestic violence, and other crimes, allowing abuse to continue unchecked. Even for citizens and legal residents, having family members with precarious status creates psychological stress and practical challenges, as mixed-status families navigate systems designed to exclude some members while including others.

Immigration enforcement itself often operates in discriminatory ways. Racial profiling in immigration enforcement leads to disproportionate stops, searches, and detention of people perceived to be Latino, regardless of their actual immigration status or citizenship. Programs like Secure Communities and 287(g), which involved local police in immigration enforcement, led to increased racial profiling and decreased trust in law enforcement within

Latino communities. The rhetoric surrounding immigration—particularly the racialization of the issue as primarily about the U.S.-Mexico border—contributes to stereotypes that affect all Latinos regardless of immigration status.

Educational Barriers

Latino students face multiple educational challenges, including segregated schools with fewer resources, language barriers, and cultural disconnects between home and school environments. These factors contribute to lower high school completion rates (82% compared to 94% for white students) and bachelor's degree attainment (21% compared to 45% for white adults).

Economic Disparities

The median household income for Latino families ($55,658 in 2020) remains significantly below that of white households ($74,912). Latino workers are overrepresented in low-wage occupations with limited benefits and protections, including agriculture, construction, and service industries. They experience higher rates of wage theft and workplace safety violations than other groups.

Healthcare Obstacles

Latinos have the highest uninsured rate of any racial or ethnic group at approximately 18%, compared to 5% for non-Hispanic whites. Language barriers, cultural differences, and limited providers in Latino neighborhoods create additional obstacles to quality care.

Language discrimination represents another dimension of systemic racism affecting Latino communities. Spanish speakers face barriers in accessing government services, healthcare, education, and employment opportunities. "English-only" policies in workplaces often target Latino employees, while accent discrimination affects even fluent English speakers. The politicization of language—with Spanish sometimes portrayed as a threat to American identity rather than an asset in a global society—creates hostility toward Latino linguistic and cultural expressions.

Housing discrimination continues to affect Latino communities, with audit studies showing that Latino home-seekers are shown fewer properties, quoted higher prices, and denied financing more often than equally qualified white home-seekers. Residential segregation concentrates many Latinos in neighborhoods with fewer resources, lower-performing schools, and more environmental hazards. During the 2008 housing crisis, predatory lending targeted Latino borrowers, leading to disproportionate foreclosure rates that erased decades of wealth accumulation.

Political representation and voting rights for Latino communities face systematic barriers. Gerrymandering has often diluted Latino voting power by splitting communities across multiple districts. Voter ID laws, restrictions on early voting, and limited language assistance disproportionately affect Latino voter participation. These barriers contribute to underrepresentation in elected office—while Latinos constitute approximately 18% of the U.S. population, they hold only about 1% of elected offices nationwide.

Addressing systemic racism affecting Latino communities requires comprehensive approaches: immigration reform that provides pathways to legal status, stronger enforcement of civil rights and labor protections, language access in essential services, investments in Latino-serving institutions, and challenging stereotypes in media and public discourse. These efforts must recognize the diversity within Latino communities while addressing the common barriers created by systemic racism.

Asian American Experience in the US System

Asian Americans have experienced distinctive patterns of systemic racism in the United States, shaped by changing geopolitical relationships, immigration policies, and racial stereotypes. While often portrayed as a "model minority" that has overcome discrimination through hard work and cultural values, this narrative obscures both historical and ongoing forms of anti-Asian racism while creating barriers to addressing persistent inequalities affecting various Asian American communities.

The history of systemic racism against Asian Americans includes some of the most explicit exclusionary policies in American history. The Chinese Exclusion Act of 1882—the first law to prohibit immigration based on nationality—banned Chinese laborers from entering the country and prevented Chinese immigrants already in the U.S. from becoming citizens. Similar restrictions were later extended to Japanese, Korean, and South Asian immigrants through the "Asiatic Barred Zone" created by the Immigration Act of 1917. These exclusions were justified through racist characterizations of Asians as unassimilable foreigners and economic threats.

Legal discrimination extended beyond immigration to affect Asian Americans' rights within the United States.

Alien land laws in western states prevented "aliens ineligible for citizenship" (a category that applied primarily to Asian immigrants) from owning property. Antimiscegenation laws prohibited marriages between whites and Asians in many states until the Supreme Court's 1967 Loving v. Virginia decision. Perhaps most egregiously, approximately 120,000 Japanese Americans—two-thirds of whom were U.S. citizens—were forcibly relocated to internment camps during World War II, losing homes, businesses, and personal property in the process.

Contemporary manifestations of anti-Asian racism range from hate crimes to more subtle forms of discrimination. The COVID-19 pandemic triggered a dramatic surge in anti-Asian violence, with the Stop AAPI Hate reporting center documenting over 10,000 incidents from March 2020 to September 2021. These incidents ranged from verbal harassment and workplace discrimination to physical assaults, reflecting the persistent stereotyping of Asian Americans as perpetual foreigners who can be blamed for international events.

The "model minority" stereotype—which characterizes Asian Americans as universally successful through hard work, strong family values, and emphasis on education—serves as a form of systemic racism by obscuring diversity within Asian American communities and the barriers they face. This stereotype pits Asian Americans against other racial minorities, implying that lack of success among other groups results from cultural deficiencies rather than structural barriers. It also creates pressure on Asian Americans to conform to expectations of academic and professional excellence while dismissing those who don't fit this narrative.

Perpetual Foreigner

Regardless of citizenship or generations in the U.S., Asian Americans are often treated as permanent outsiders

Model Minority

Expectations of universal success ignore diversity and structural barriers within Asian American communities

Yellow Peril

During times of international tension, Asian Americans are portrayed as economic or security threats

Invisibility

Asian American perspectives and experiences are frequently excluded from broader discussions of race

The aggregation of diverse populations under the "Asian American" category masks significant disparities among different ethnic groups. While some Asian American groups have high average incomes and educational attainment, others face substantial economic challenges. Hmong, Cambodian, Laotian, and Burmese Americans have poverty rates significantly higher than the national average. These disparities reflect different immigration histories, including refugee experiences, as well as linguistic isolation and limited access to culturally appropriate services.

In employment, Asian Americans face a "bamboo ceiling" that limits advancement to leadership positions despite high levels of education and representation in professional roles. Asian Americans are the least likely racial group to be promoted to management positions relative to their representation in the professional workforce. Stereotypes about Asian Americans as technically proficient but lacking leadership qualities contribute to this pattern of exclusion from executive ranks.

Addressing systemic racism affecting Asian Americans requires recognizing both historical injustices and contemporary barriers, disaggregating data to identify disparities among different ethnic groups, challenging harmful stereotypes, increasing representation in decision-making positions, and incorporating Asian American experiences in broader discussions of race and racism. It also requires solidarity across racial groups to resist efforts to use the "model minority" narrative to undermine anti-racism work more broadly.

Colorism and Internalized Oppression

Colorism refers to discrimination based on skin tone, where lighter skin is privileged over darker skin, even within the same racial or ethnic group. As a distinct but related phenomenon to racism, colorism represents a complex dimension of racial hierarchy that reinforces white supremacist standards while simultaneously dividing communities of color from within.

Historical Roots

The historical origins of colorism in the United States trace back to slavery, where enslavers often assigned lighter-skinned enslaved people to house labor and darker-skinned individuals to field labor. This deliberate stratification created economic and social advantages based on proximity to whiteness that have persisted through generations.

Global Manifestations

While American colorism emerged through the specific context of chattel slavery and Jim Crow, similar hierarchies exist globally, influenced by European colonialism, caste systems, and indigenous social structures. Across diverse societies, lighter skin has been associated with higher social status, wealth, and desirability.

Internalized Oppression

Colorism functions as both external discrimination and internalized oppression, where communities adopt and perpetuate color hierarchies through family dynamics, social interactions, and cultural preferences. This internalization complicates addressing colorism as solely an external system of oppression.

Economic Impact

Research consistently demonstrates that darker-skinned individuals face wage penalties compared to their lighter-skinned counterparts of the same race. Studies show that the "skin tone penalty" can be as significant as the racial wage gap itself, with darker-skinned Black Americans earning up to 25% less than those with lighter skin tones, even when controlling for education and background.

Criminal Justice

Within the criminal justice system, colorism manifests in harsher sentencing for darker-skinned defendants. Research indicates that darker-skinned Black defendants receive sentences approximately 20% longer than those with lighter skin tones who committed identical crimes, demonstrating how skin tone discrimination operates even within racial categories.

Media Representation

Entertainment and advertising industries have historically favored lighter-skinned people of color for leading roles and mainstream marketing. This pattern reinforces beauty standards that privilege proximity to whiteness while limiting representation of darker-skinned individuals, particularly women, to stereotypical or background roles.

Education

Studies have documented that darker-skinned students face higher rates of discipline and lower teacher expectations compared to their lighter-skinned peers. These biases contribute to educational disparities that follow students through their academic careers and into professional life.

Intersectionality and Impact

Colorism intersects powerfully with gender, creating particularly harmful effects for darker-skinned women who face both racial and gender discrimination compounded by skin tone bias. This intersection manifests in marriage markets, employment opportunities, and media representation, with studies showing darker-skinned women earning less, facing higher rates of exclusion, and experiencing more significant mental health impacts from discrimination.

While colorism creates hierarchies within communities of color, it ultimately reinforces white nationalism by dividing potential solidarity and maintaining proximity to whiteness as the standard for acceptance and success. Any comprehensive approach to dismantling systemic racism must address colorism as both a symptom and perpetuating mechanism of racial hierarchy in American society.

Contemporary Resistance

Recent movements toward celebrating darker skin tones, natural hair, and diverse beauty standards represent important resistance to colorism. Social media campaigns, consumer activism targeting beauty and fashion industries, and educational initiatives have created platforms for challenging colorist ideologies and practices. However, addressing the structural elements of colorism requires sustained policy attention to discrimination in employment, housing, education, criminal justice, and media representation.

How Systemic Racism Persists: Institutional Inertia

Despite formal legal equality and widespread condemnation of explicit racism, systemic racism persists through mechanisms of institutional inertia—the tendency of established systems and practices to continue operating in ways that produce racial disparities even without conscious discriminatory intent. Understanding these mechanisms helps explain why racial inequality has proven so durable even as explicit racial attitudes have generally improved over time.

"Colorblind" policies often perpetuate racial inequality by ignoring the context of historical discrimination and ongoing disparities. When policies are designed without considering how race shapes opportunity and resources, they frequently reproduce existing inequalities. For example, school funding formulas based on local property taxes appear race-neutral but generate dramatically unequal resources for schools serving different racial populations due to residential segregation and wealth disparities with roots in explicitly racist policies. Similarly, "race-neutral" college admissions criteria like standardized test scores and legacy preferences disproportionately advantage white applicants due to unequal K-12 education and historical exclusion of people of color from elite institutions.

Organizational cultures and "standard operating procedures" often embed racial biases that persist independently of individual intentions. Hiring practices that rely on employee referrals or recruitment from particular schools tend to reproduce the existing racial composition of organizations. Subjective evaluation criteria allow unconscious biases to influence decisions about promotions, discipline, and resource allocation. Even technological systems like algorithms used in hiring, lending, healthcare, and criminal justice frequently incorporate racial biases from the historical data used to train them, creating automated discrimination that appears objective but reproduces patterns of inequality.

Feedback loops between different domains of inequality create self-reinforcing systems that maintain racial stratification across generations. Housing segregation affects school quality, which influences educational outcomes, which shape employment opportunities, which determine housing options—creating a cycle that reproduces inequality without requiring ongoing explicit discrimination. Similarly, concentrated disadvantage in particular neighborhoods leads to reduced services, lower property values, and disinvestment, which further concentrate disadvantage in a self-reinforcing pattern.

Individual adaptations to discrimination can inadvertently reinforce systemic patterns. When people of color anticipate discrimination in certain fields or institutions, they may avoid these spaces—a rational response that nevertheless results in continued segregation and lack of diversity. When parents make educational choices to protect their children from hostile environments, these choices can lead to increased segregation. These adaptations are reasonable responses to racism, but they can have the unintended consequence of maintaining systems of inequality.

Formal Equality

Laws prohibit explicit discrimination but fail to address structural barriers or remedy historical injustice

Colorblind Ideology

Focus on individual merit without acknowledging how race shapes opportunity preserves existing advantages

Self-Reinforcing Systems

Disadvantages in one domain create barriers in others, creating cycles that persist across generations

Institutional Resistance

Organizations resist changes that would redistribute resources or opportunities more equitably

Institutional resistance to equity-focused reforms represents another mechanism of persistence. When policies are proposed to address racial disparities—whether through affirmative action, school integration, or targeted investments in disadvantaged communities—they often face significant opposition from those who benefit from the status quo. This resistance is frequently framed in race-neutral terms emphasizing meritocracy, local control, or individual rights, obscuring how maintaining current systems preserves racial advantages and disadvantages.

The cumulative disadvantage produced by these mechanisms creates barriers that individual effort alone cannot overcome. When systemic barriers limit access to quality education, safe housing, healthcare, and employment opportunities across generations, the resulting disparities in resources and opportunities cannot be attributed simply to individual choices or capabilities. Understanding systemic racism as a product of institutional inertia rather than merely individual prejudice helps explain its persistence and points toward the need for structural rather than merely interpersonal solutions.

Data and the Measurement of Racial Inequities

Quantifying racial disparities through data collection and analysis plays a crucial role in identifying, understanding, and addressing systemic racism. While statistics alone cannot capture the full lived experience of racism, they provide essential evidence of patterns that extend beyond individual anecdotes, helping to document the scope of racial inequality and track progress or regression over time. However, the processes of defining, collecting, and interpreting racial data themselves reflect power dynamics that can either illuminate or obscure important aspects of racial inequality.

A wide range of indicators consistently reveal racial disparities across domains of American life. In economics, data on income, wealth, unemployment, and poverty show persistent gaps between racial groups. In education, statistics on test scores, graduation rates, disciplinary actions, and college completion document unequal outcomes. Criminal justice data reveal disparities in arrests, sentencing, and incarceration rates. Health indicators show gaps in insurance coverage, disease prevalence, and mortality rates. Housing data demonstrate segregation, homeownership differences, and valuation disparities. These statistics constitute a powerful empirical foundation for understanding systemic racism as a structural rather than merely interpersonal phenomenon.

However, the collection and interpretation of racial data face significant challenges. The very categories used to classify people by race have changed over time and continue to evolve, reflecting the social construction of race rather than biological reality. The Census Bureau has repeatedly revised its racial categories, most recently adding the option to select multiple races in 2000. These changing classifications complicate historical comparisons and may not align with how individuals identify themselves or experience discrimination.

Data gaps present another significant challenge. Some important aspects of racial inequality remain poorly measured or not measured at all. For example, comprehensive national data on police use of force by race has historically been limited, hampering efforts to address disparities in policing. Similarly, data on discrimination in hiring, housing, and lending often relies on audit studies or complaint statistics rather than comprehensive measurement. These gaps sometimes reflect political decisions about what information is worth collecting and what remains invisible in official statistics.

Even when data exists, disaggregation issues can mask important patterns. Broad racial categories like "Asian American" or "Hispanic/Latino" aggregate diverse populations with significantly different experiences and outcomes. Without disaggregation, the specific challenges facing subgroups can remain hidden. For example, educational and economic outcomes vary substantially among different Asian American ethnic groups, but this variation disappears when data is reported only for the aggregate category.

The interpretation of racial disparity data raises additional complexities. When disparities are documented, competing explanations emerge: Do disparities reflect discrimination, historical legacies, cultural differences, or other factors? Research designs that can isolate the specific contribution of discrimination from other variables are difficult to implement, especially for studying systemic rather than individual discrimination. This interpretive flexibility allows those invested in denying racism to attribute disparities to non-racial factors, even when evidence of discrimination is strong.

Despite these challenges, data remains essential for addressing systemic racism. Comprehensive, disaggregated data collection with appropriate privacy protections enables identification of problem areas, development of targeted interventions, and evaluation of policy effectiveness. In recent years, some jurisdictions have implemented racial equity impact assessments that systematically analyze how policies affect different racial groups before implementation. Similarly, improved methods for measuring discrimination through audit studies, controlled experiments, and sophisticated statistical analyses help distinguish discriminatory patterns from other sources of disparity.

Moving forward, improving the quality, comprehensiveness, and accessibility of racial equity data represents a crucial step in addressing systemic racism. This includes expanding data collection in understudied areas, increasing disaggregation to capture within-group diversity, developing better measures of systemic and institutional (rather than merely individual) discrimination, and ensuring that affected communities have input into how data about them is collected, interpreted, and used.

Case Study: The Flint Water Crisis

The Flint water crisis represents one of the most egregious examples of environmental injustice and systemic racism in recent American history. Beginning in 2014, residents of Flint, Michigan—a majority-Black city where over 40% of residents live below the poverty line—were exposed to dangerous levels of lead and other contaminants in their drinking water, resulting in a public health emergency with long-lasting consequences. The crisis illuminates how race and class shape governmental decision-making, resource allocation, and official responses to community concerns.

The crisis began in April 2014 when, under the direction of a state-appointed emergency manager, Flint switched its water source from Lake Huron (via the Detroit Water and Sewerage Department) to the Flint River as a cost-cutting measure. Crucially, officials failed to add corrosion inhibitors to the more corrosive river water. This decision allowed lead from aging pipes to leach into the drinking water, exposing thousands of residents to dangerous levels of the neurotoxin, which is particularly harmful to children's developing brains.

Almost immediately, residents began complaining about discolored, foul-smelling water and reporting health problems including rashes, hair loss, and respiratory issues. These complaints were repeatedly dismissed by city and state officials, who insisted the water was safe despite mounting evidence to the contrary. When residents—predominantly working-class Black citizens—organized to demand accountability, they were often treated with condescension and skepticism by authorities. It took the involvement of outside experts, including Dr. Mona Hanna-Attisha, who documented elevated blood lead levels in Flint children, and EPA whistleblower Miguel Del Toral, before officials finally acknowledged the crisis in late 2015, over 18 months after the initial switch.

The racial dimensions of the crisis are inescapable. A state-commissioned Civil Rights Commission report concluded that "race was a factor in the Flint water crisis" and that the slow response resulted in part from "systemic racism that was built into the foundation and growth of Flint, its industry and the suburban area surrounding it." The emergency manager law itself disproportionately affected majority-Black cities, effectively removing democratic control from communities of color. Would the same decisions have been made, and would complaints have been ignored for so long, in a predominantly white, affluent community? Historical patterns suggest otherwise.

April 2014

Flint switches water source to Flint River without proper corrosion control treatment

January-February 2015

High levels of lead and carcinogens detected; state begins delivering bottled water to government buildings while telling residents tap water is safe

September 2015

Dr. Mona Hanna-Attisha publicly reveals elevated blood lead levels in Flint children

October 2015

Flint reconnects to Detroit water system, but damaged pipes continue to leach lead

January 2016

State of emergency declared; National Guard distributes bottled water

The health impacts of the crisis have been severe and long-lasting. Lead exposure can cause developmental delays, behavioral problems, and reduced IQ in children, with effects that may not be fully apparent for years. Flint also experienced an outbreak of Legionnaires' disease linked to the water change, resulting in at least 12 deaths. The psychological trauma of the crisis—including anxiety about health effects, anger at government betrayal, and stress from daily struggles to obtain safe water—has created lasting mental health impacts in the community.

Accountability for the crisis has been limited and delayed. While some officials faced criminal charges, many cases were later dismissed or resolved through plea agreements to lesser charges. A $626 million settlement for victims was approved in 2021, but many residents feel this is inadequate given the long-term health impacts and property damage. The work of replacing all lead service lines in Flint continues, with completion initially promised by 2020 but still ongoing as of the date of this publication.

The Flint water crisis demonstrates how systemic racism operates through seemingly race-neutral decisions about resource allocation, infrastructure investment, and governmental responsiveness. It reveals how the voices and concerns of predominantly Black communities are often discounted or dismissed by authorities, and how environmental burdens are disproportionately placed on communities with less political power. The crisis has become a symbol of environmental injustice in America and a stark reminder of how race continues to influence which communities receive protection from environmental hazards and which are left vulnerable.

Case Study: COVID-19 Pandemic Impacts

The COVID-19 pandemic exposed and exacerbated existing racial inequalities in American society, creating a natural experiment that revealed how systemic racism shapes health outcomes, economic security, and access to resources during a crisis. The disproportionate impact of the pandemic on communities of color provides a contemporary case study of how historical inequities and current structural barriers combine to produce racialized outcomes even in the absence of explicitly discriminatory intent.

Health disparities emerged early in the pandemic and persisted throughout. Black, Hispanic/Latino, and Native American populations experienced significantly higher rates of COVID-19 infection, hospitalization, and death compared to white Americans. According to CDC data, Black Americans were 2.6 times more likely to be hospitalized and 1.9 times more likely to die from COVID-19 than white Americans. Hispanic/Latino Americans faced 2.5 times higher hospitalization rates and 2.1 times higher death rates. Native Americans experienced the highest disparities, with 3.3 times higher hospitalization and 2.2 times higher death rates than whites.

These disparities reflected multiple dimensions of systemic racism. Residential segregation concentrated people of color in densely populated areas where the virus spread more easily. Occupational segregation meant Black and Latino workers were overrepresented in "essential" jobs that couldn't be performed remotely, increasing their exposure risk. Limited access to healthcare, including higher uninsured rates and fewer healthcare facilities in minority neighborhoods, created barriers to testing and treatment. Underlying health conditions associated with environmental racism and healthcare inequities—including asthma, diabetes, and hypertension—increased vulnerability to severe COVID-19 outcomes.

Economic impacts were similarly unequal. Job losses were concentrated in service industries where workers of color are overrepresented, while white-collar jobs that could transition to remote work were more likely to be held by white workers. According to Bureau of Labor Statistics data, unemployment rates during the early pandemic peaked at 16.8% for Black workers and 18.9% for Hispanic workers, compared to 14.2% for white workers. Even as the economy recovered, racial gaps in unemployment persisted. Small businesses owned by people of color closed at higher rates due to limited cash reserves, reduced access to banking relationships, and initial disadvantages in accessing Paycheck Protection Program loans.

Educational disruptions disproportionately affected students of color. Schools serving predominantly minority students were less likely to have resources for effective remote learning, including adequate technology, internet access, and support services. Many students in these communities lacked home computers or reliable internet connections, creating a "digital divide" that impeded educational progress. Parents of color were less likely to have jobs that allowed them to work from home and supervise remote learning, forcing difficult choices between economic security and educational support.

Vaccine access and hesitancy revealed additional dimensions of racial inequality. Initial vaccine distribution sites were often concentrated in whiter, more affluent areas with better transportation access. Many vaccination systems relied on internet-based registration that created barriers for those with limited digital access or English proficiency. While hesitancy existed across all racial groups, it stemmed from different sources—for communities of color, hesitancy often reflected rational concerns based on historical medical abuses and ongoing experiences of discrimination in healthcare settings.

Government responses frequently failed to adequately address these disparities. Early testing sites were disproportionately located in whiter, more affluent areas despite higher case rates in minority communities. Data collection on racial impacts was initially limited and inconsistent across jurisdictions, hampering targeted response efforts. Economic relief programs, while significant, were not designed to address the specific barriers facing workers and businesses in communities of color, including limited banking relationships and documentation challenges for immigrant families.

The COVID-19 pandemic demonstrates how systemic racism operates during a crisis, channeling both harms and resources along racial lines even without explicit discrimination. The pandemic did not create these inequalities but rather revealed and amplified existing structural disparities in health, economics, education, and access to resources. As the nation continues to recover from the pandemic, addressing these disparities requires not only universal policies but targeted approaches that recognize and remedy the specific barriers facing communities of color.

Myths Debunked: Progress and Remaining Barriers

Discussions of systemic racism often encounter a set of persistent myths and misconceptions that obscure both the progress that has been made and the substantial barriers that remain. These narratives frequently minimize the ongoing impact of racial inequality while placing responsibility primarily on individuals rather than systems. By examining and debunking these myths, we can develop a more accurate understanding of the current state of racial equity in America.

Myth: Systemic racism ended due to the civil rights movement

This perhaps the most pervasive myth. It suggests that the civil rights movement effectively ended racism, making contemporary racial disparities primarily the result of individual choices rather than systemic barriers. This narrative points to landmark achievements like Brown v. Board of Education (1954), the Civil Rights Act of 1964, and the Voting Rights Act of 1965 as having created a level playing field where explicit discrimination is illegal and opportunity is equally available to all. While these legal changes did represent significant progress, they addressed only the most overt forms of discrimination while leaving many structural barriers intact. School segregation, for instance, has actually increased in recent decades despite legal prohibition, while the economic legacy of centuries of discrimination was never systematically addressed.

Myth: Socioeconomic status, not race, determines opportunity and outcomes

This framing argues that while racial disparities exist, they primarily reflect class differences rather than racial discrimination per se. However, research consistently demonstrates that racial disparities persist even when controlling for socioeconomic status. Middle-class Black families have approximately one-eighth the wealth of middle-class white families. Black college graduates face higher unemployment rates than white high school graduates. Studies of hiring, housing, and lending consistently find discrimination against middle-class applicants of color. While class certainly matters, it does not erase the independent effects of race.

Myth: Colorblindness is the solution to racism

The belief that ignoring race entirely—treating everyone "the same" regardless of racial identity—represents the best approach to achieving racial equality. This framework fails to recognize how race-neutral policies can produce racially unequal outcomes when implemented within existing structures of inequality.

Myth: Individual success stories disprove systemic racism

The argument that successful individuals from minority groups demonstrate that systemic barriers don't exist or can be overcome through personal effort alone. This reasoning confuses exceptions with norms and ignores how systemic barriers create unequal probabilities of success rather than absolute impossibility.

Myth: Racial disparities reflect cultural differences

The claim that disparities in education, employment, income, and other outcomes primarily reflect cultural values or behaviors rather than structural barriers. This narrative ignores substantial evidence of discrimination and structural disadvantage while attributing complex social patterns to stereotyped cultural traits.

The "model minority" myth applied to Asian Americans represents another damaging narrative in discussions of racism. This framework portrays Asian Americans as universally successful through cultural values of hard work, family cohesion, and educational emphasis, implicitly suggesting that other minority groups could achieve similar success if they adopted similar values. This narrative obscures the diversity within Asian American communities, many of which face significant economic challenges. It ignores how immigration selectivity has shaped Asian American demographics, with many immigrants arriving with educational advantages. Perhaps most problematically, it uses one minority group to invalidate the experiences of others, reinforcing a framework that attributes racial disparities to cultural deficiencies rather than structural barriers.

Discussions of progress often focus exclusively on individual attitudes, noting reduced explicit racial prejudice over time as evidence that racism is declining. While changes in attitudes do represent meaningful progress, this framing conflates individual prejudice with systemic racism. Systems and institutions can produce racially unequal outcomes regardless of the conscious intentions of individuals within them. Housing segregation, wealth inequality, and educational disparities can persist through institutional inertia even as individual attitudes improve.

Perhaps the most fundamental myth is that addressing systemic racism requires proving malicious intent or identifying specific "racists" responsible for creating disparities. This framework misunderstands how systems operate, focusing on individual culpability rather than collective responsibility for changing structures that produce harmful outcomes. Many aspects of systemic racism function through policies and practices that appear race-neutral but produce racially disparate results when implemented within existing structures of inequality.

By examining these myths critically, we can develop a more accurate understanding of both progress and persistent barriers. Significant advances have been made in legal protections, representation in various fields, and reduction of explicit prejudice. However, substantial structural barriers remain embedded in housing, education, criminal justice, healthcare, and other systems. Addressing these barriers requires moving beyond individual blame to develop systemic solutions that actively promote equity rather than passively perpetuating historical patterns of advantage and disadvantage.

The Role of Grassroots Activism

Throughout American history, grassroots activism has been the primary driver of progress toward racial justice, challenging systemic racism when institutional channels have failed to deliver change. From abolition to civil rights to contemporary movements, organized community activism has pushed reluctant systems toward greater equity and accountability. Understanding this history illuminates both successful strategies for creating change and the ongoing importance of collective action in addressing systemic racism.

The modern civil rights movement provides a powerful example of effective grassroots organizing against entrenched racial oppression. While often remembered through iconic figures like Dr. Martin Luther King Jr., the movement's strength came from thousands of ordinary people who participated in boycotts, sit-ins, freedom rides, and voting rights campaigns. Organizations like the Southern Christian Leadership Conference (SCLC),

Student Nonviolent Coordinating Committee (SNCC), and National Association for the Advancement of Colored People (NAACP) developed sophisticated strategies combining direct action, legal challenges, economic pressure, and moral appeals to dismantle segregation and secure voting rights.

These activists faced violent resistance, including police brutality, vigilante attacks, economic retaliation, and assassination. The bombing of Birmingham's 16th Street Baptist Church in 1963, killing four young girls, and the murders of civil rights workers James Chaney, Andrew Goodman, and Michael Schwerner in Mississippi in 1964 represent just two examples of the violence directed at racial justice activists. Despite these dangers, the movement's persistence ultimately produced landmark legislation including the Civil Rights Act of 1964 and the Voting Rights Act of 1965.

Contemporary movements have built on this legacy while developing new strategies adapted to current contexts. Black Lives Matter emerged in 2013 following the acquittal of George Zimmerman in the killing of Trayvon Martin, gaining prominence during protests over the police killings of Michael Brown in Ferguson, Missouri and Eric Garner in New York. Unlike earlier movements with centralized leadership, BLM operates as a decentralized network of activists united by shared principles and hashtags. This structure has enabled rapid mobilization across multiple locations while making the movement resilient against attempts to silence individual leaders.

Social media has transformed modern activism, enabling movements to bypass traditional media gatekeepers and communicate directly with supporters and the broader public. Viral videos of police violence have made visible abuses that might previously have gone undocumented, while hashtags like #BlackLivesMatter and #SayHerName create frameworks for understanding individual incidents as part of broader patterns. These technologies have facilitated rapid mobilization and connection of local organizing to national and global movements.

1955-1956

Montgomery Bus Boycott launches modern civil rights movement after Rosa Parks' arrest

1960

Greensboro sit-ins begin when four Black students request service at whites-only lunch counter

1963

March on Washington draws 250,000 people; Martin Luther King Jr. delivers "I Have a Dream" speech

2013-2014

Black Lives Matter movement emerges following acquittal of George Zimmerman and Ferguson protests

2020

Murder of George Floyd catalyzes global protests estimated to involve 15-26 million people in the U.S. alone

Local organizing remains essential to addressing systemic racism, even when less visible than national movements. Community organizations work to address specific manifestations of racial inequality in housing, education, policing, environmental justice, and other domains. Groups like the Texas Organizing Project in Houston, POWER in Philadelphia, and Community Coalition in Los Angeles build power among residents of color to influence local policies on issues from school funding to affordable housing to police accountability. These organizations recognize that while national policy changes are important, many decisions that directly affect communities of color occur at municipal and county levels.

The murders of George Floyd, Breonna Taylor, and others in 2020 catalyzed what may have been the largest protest movement in American history, with an estimated 15-26 million people participating in demonstrations across all 50 states. These protests produced concrete changes in many jurisdictions, including police department reforms, reallocation of resources from policing to community services, removal of Confederate monuments, and increased corporate commitments to diversity and inclusion. However, the movement also faced backlash, including legislative efforts to criminalize protest tactics and ban teaching about systemic racism in schools.

The history of racial justice activism demonstrates both the power of organized communities to create change and the persistent resistance to racial equity. Progress has never been linear or automatic but has required sustained pressure from those most affected by injustice. As contemporary movements continue this legacy, they face both new opportunities created by technology and communication tools and new challenges in translating widespread awareness into lasting structural change. The continued necessity of grassroots activism itself reflects the persistence of systemic racism that institutional channels have failed to dismantle.

Government and Judicial Responses

Government institutions—including legislatures, executive agencies, and courts—have played complex and sometimes contradictory roles in addressing systemic racism. While these institutions have sometimes acted to dismantle discriminatory systems, they have also frequently preserved racial hierarchies or limited remedies for historical injustices. This mixed record reflects broader societal tensions around race and the responsiveness of democratic institutions to different constituencies.

The judiciary, particularly the Supreme Court, has issued landmark decisions that both advanced and impeded racial justice. Brown v. Board of Education (1954) overturned the "separate but equal" doctrine established in Plessy v. Ferguson (1896), declaring segregated public schools unconstitutional and providing a legal foundation for dismantling Jim Crow segregation. Loving v. Virginia (1967) struck down anti-miscegenation laws that prohibited interracial marriage. More recently, Texas Department of Housing v. Inclusive Communities Project (2015) upheld the use of disparate impact theory in establishing housing discrimination claims, recognizing that policies can be discriminatory in effect even without discriminatory intent.

However, the Supreme Court has also issued decisions that have limited efforts to address systemic racism. Milliken v. Bradley (1974) effectively halted metropolitan school desegregation by prohibiting integration plans that crossed district lines, allowing white flight to suburban districts to maintain segregation. Regents of the University of California v. Bakke (1978) placed significant constraints on affirmative action in higher education. Most recently, Students for Fair Admissions v. Harvard (2023) effectively prohibited race-conscious admissions policies in higher education, reversing decades of precedent allowing limited consideration of race to promote diversity.

Landmark Civil Rights Legislation

- **Civil Rights Act of 1964**: Prohibited discrimination in public accommodations, employment, and federally funded programs
- **Voting Rights Act of 1965**: Banned discriminatory voting practices and established federal oversight of election procedures in states with histories of discrimination
- **Fair Housing Act of 1968**: Prohibited discrimination in housing sales, rentals, and financing
- Americans with Disabilities Act of 1990: Protected individuals with disabilities from discrimination

Significant Court Limitations

- **Shelby County v. Holder (2013):** Struck down key provisions of the Voting Rights Act requiring federal preclearance of election changes in states with histories of discrimination
- **McCleskey v. Kemp (1987)**: Rejected statistical evidence of racial disparities in death penalty application as insufficient to prove discrimination
- **Washington v. Davis (1976)**: Established that claims of racial discrimination under the Equal Protection Clause require proof of discriminatory intent, not just disparate impact

- **Students for Fair Admissions v. Harvard (2023)**: Prohibited consideration of race in college admissions

Perhaps most consequentially, Shelby County v. Holder (2013) invalidated key provisions of the Voting Rights Act that required federal preclearance for changes to election procedures in jurisdictions with histories of discrimination. Following this decision, many states implemented new voting restrictions that disproportionately affected minority voters, including strict voter ID requirements, purges of voter rolls, and reductions in early voting opportunities.

Legislative responses to systemic racism have similarly shown mixed results. The Civil Rights Act of 1964, Voting Rights Act of 1965, and Fair Housing Act of 1968 represented landmark achievements in prohibiting explicit discrimination. However, enforcement of these laws has been inconsistent, and they primarily addressed overt discrimination rather than more subtle structural barriers or remedies for historical injustices. More recent legislative efforts to address racial equity, such as the George Floyd Justice in Policing Act, have often stalled due to partisan polarization and competing priorities.

Actions taken by the executive branch have fluctuated significantly between administrations. The Obama administration introduced measures aimed at tackling systemic racism in areas such as criminal justice, housing, and education. This included conducting investigations into police departments with histories of civil rights violations and providing guidance to help reduce racial disparities in school discipline. In contrast, the first Trump administration rolled back many of these policies, curtailing civil rights enforcement and limiting diversity training within federal agencies and contractors. The Biden administration re-emphasized racial equity through a series of executive orders and agency initiatives. Meanwhile, the second Trump administration sought to intensify and codify many of the earlier efforts to dismantle the initiatives established by both the Obama and Biden administrations.

State and local governments have sometimes led innovation in addressing systemic racism. Some jurisdictions have implemented reforms in policing, including restrictions on use of force, civilian oversight bodies, and reallocation of resources to alternative response models. Cities like Evanston, Illinois and states like California have explored reparations programs for specific historical injustices. However, other states have moved in opposite directions, enacting laws restricting voting access, limiting discussions of racism in schools, and preempting local civil rights ordinances.

The uneven government response to systemic racism reflects broader political and social dynamics. Periods of progress have typically followed sustained pressure from social movements rather than emerging independently from government institutions. The effectiveness of government responses has been limited by competing priorities, ideological differences about the role of government in addressing racial inequality, and the influence of constituencies that benefit from existing arrangements. As a result, while government action has been essential to civil rights advances, it has rarely been sufficient without continued advocacy and accountability from affected communities and their allies.

Corporate America and DEI Initiatives

The business sector represents another arena where responses to systemic racism have evolved significantly in recent decades. From the civil rights era's focus on basic non-discrimination to contemporary Diversity, Equity, and Inclusion (DEI) initiatives, corporate approaches have expanded in scope and ambition while also generating significant controversy and backlash. These efforts reflect both genuine commitments to racial equity and strategic responses to changing social expectations, market pressures, and legal requirements.

The modern corporate DEI movement has roots in affirmative action policies of the 1960s and 1970s, which initially focused on compliance with Equal Employment Opportunity (EEO) requirements established by the Civil Rights Act of 1964. These early efforts primarily aimed to avoid discrimination claims through standardized hiring procedures and modest diversity goals. By the 1980s and 1990s, the "business case for diversity" emerged as companies recognized potential competitive advantages in diverse workforces, including access to broader talent pools, improved decision-making, and better connections to diverse consumer markets.

Contemporary DEI initiatives have expanded beyond compliance and representation to address more systemic aspects of corporate culture and operations. Many companies have established dedicated DEI offices with significant budgets and executive leadership positions like Chief Diversity Officer. These expanded programs typically include recruitment initiatives targeting underrepresented groups, mentorship and development programs to support advancement of employees of color, cultural competence training, employee resource groups, and supplier diversity efforts to increase procurement from minority-owned businesses.

The 2020 racial justice protests following George Floyd's murder catalyzed unprecedented corporate commitments to racial equity. Major companies pledged billions of dollars toward racial justice initiatives, including investments in Black-owned businesses, financial institutions serving minority communities, and philanthropic support for civil rights organizations. Many publicly committed to specific representation goals and greater transparency in diversity metrics. These commitments represented a significant departure from previous approaches that often treated racism as a historical issue rather than an ongoing structural challenge requiring active intervention.

Common Corporate DEI Elements

- Diverse recruitment pipelines and hiring practices
- Employee resource groups for underrepresented communities
- Bias and cultural competence training
- Mentorship and sponsorship programs
- Pay equity analysis and remediation

Limitations and Critiques

- Focus on representation without addressing structural issues
- Insufficient accountability mechanisms for goals
- Training programs with limited evidence of effectiveness

- Tension between public commitments and internal practices
- Vulnerability to political backlash and "DEI fatigue"

Emerging Best Practices

- Data-driven approaches with transparent metrics
- Integration of equity principles into core business operations
- Executive compensation tied to diversity outcomes
- External partnerships with minority-serving institutions
- Regular equity audits of policies and practices

Despite these expanded efforts, corporate DEI initiatives face significant limitations and critiques from multiple perspectives. Many programs emphasize diversity in representation without addressing deeper structural issues like corporate culture, decision-making processes, or business models that may perpetuate inequality. Employee training programs, while common, show mixed evidence of effectiveness in reducing bias or changing behaviors. Leadership remains predominantly white and male at most major corporations, particularly at the highest levels—in 2021, only 8% of Fortune 500 CEOs were people of color, and fewer than 1% were Black.

Critics from the political left often characterize corporate DEI efforts as superficial "diversity washing" that provides positive publicity without meaningful change in power structures or economic inequality. Meanwhile, conservative critics have increasingly targeted DEI initiatives as promoting "reverse discrimination" or ideological conformity. This political backlash has intensified since 2021, with some states enacting legislation restricting DEI training or investment considerations in public institutions and contracts.

During his first term, President Donald Trump initiated efforts to dismantle DEI initiatives, and during his return to the White House he continued this agenda.

In an address to Congress, Trump declared that his administration has eliminated DEI policies across the federal government, the private sector, and the military, asserting, "Our country will be woke no longer."

Immediately after his second inauguration, Trump issued executive orders targeting DEI programs, urging federal contractors to end "illegal DEI discrimination" and requesting lists of companies with DEI policies for potential investigations.

Defense Secretary Pete Hegseth reinforced this stance with a directive to Pentagon staff reading "DoD ≠ DEI," warning non-compliant employees they would be dismissed. Some companies, like Target and Meta, scrapped DEI programs to align with Trump's administration.

Andrea Abrams, executive director of Defending American Values Coalition, criticized Trump's actions, stating, "His baseless attacks on DEI undermine the promise of America." With Trump leading the charge, tensions over DEI in the nation remain high.

Evaluating the effectiveness of corporate DEI (Diversity, Equity, and Inclusion) initiatives in combatting systemic racism presents a significant challenge. The actions taken by Trump and his administration have further complicated corporations' efforts to rectify past injustices. While some companies have made notable strides in diversifying their workforce and leadership, fostering inclusive cultures, and allocating resources to historically marginalized communities, others have found it difficult to convert their public pledges into measurable results or lasting change. The most successful strategies involve embedding equity considerations into the core operations of the business rather than treating DEI as an isolated effort. These strategies also incorporate clear accountability mechanisms for achieving goals, leverage data to pinpoint and tackle specific obstacles, and engage employees at all levels in both the development and implementation of solutions.

As corporations grapple with these complex challenges, their strategies are likely to be influenced by a variety of factors, including pressure from employees, consumers, and investors; changes in legal regulations; competitive landscapes in talent acquisition; shifting political loyalties; and broader social and political movements. The struggle between viewing diversity, equity, and inclusion (DEI) as a moral obligation versus a business tactic will continue to shape how companies define and implement these initiatives. Ultimately, corporate America's effectiveness in tackling systemic racism hinges not only on specific programs and policies but also on deeper questions regarding the purpose of business and its obligations to society that extend beyond simply maximizing profits. With the federal government increasingly seen as an inconsistent role model, DEI is poised to either transform into something new or become undermined by its own ideals.

The Role of Education in Remediation

Education has long been viewed as both a site where systemic racism operates and a potential catalyst for dismantling it. Schools and universities simultaneously reproduce racial hierarchies through unequal resources and opportunities while also offering spaces where critical thinking about race and racism can develop. Educational approaches to addressing systemic racism include curriculum reform, pedagogical innovations, institutional policy changes, and broader efforts to create more equitable educational systems.

Curriculum that explicitly addresses racism and racial justice has evolved significantly over time. Early multicultural education often focused on cultural celebrations and contributions of different groups, sometimes criticized as a "heroes and holidays" approach that highlighted exceptional individuals without examining systemic issues. More recent approaches emphasize critical analysis of how racism has shaped American institutions and history, examining not just individual prejudice but structural forms of discrimination and their lasting consequences. These approaches include ethnic studies programs, which research suggests can improve academic outcomes for students of all backgrounds while particularly benefiting students of color.

Teaching about systemic racism requires developmentally appropriate approaches across different educational levels. In early childhood, anti-bias education focuses on helping young children recognize and respect differences while challenging stereotypes they may already have absorbed from media and social environments. Middle and high school curricula can incorporate more complex historical analysis and critical media literacy to help students understand how racism operates systemically. Higher education offers opportunities for deeper exploration of theoretical frameworks and discipline-specific manifestations of racial inequality.

Culturally responsive education represents another important educational approach to addressing racism. This framework, developed by scholars like Gloria Ladson-Billings and Geneva Gay, emphasizes teaching methods that connect to students' cultural backgrounds and lived experiences. Rather than treating students of color as deficient or requiring assimilation to dominant cultural norms, culturally responsive pedagogy builds on the cultural knowledge and perspectives students bring to the classroom. Research indicates that these approaches can increase engagement, improve academic outcomes, and develop positive racial identities among students of color while helping all students develop cross-cultural competence.

Knowledge

Understanding historical and contemporary manifestations of racism across different domains

Awareness

Recognizing how one's own identity and position shape perspectives on race

Skills

Developing abilities to communicate across differences and identify/address inequities

Action

Applying anti-racist principles in personal behavior and institutional practices

Institutional approaches to addressing racism in education include policy reforms and structural changes. Universities have implemented more holistic admissions processes that consider the context of students' achievements rather than relying solely on standardized metrics that correlate with socioeconomic advantage. K-12 districts have reformed disciplinary policies to reduce racial disparities in suspensions and expulsions. Faculty hiring initiatives have aimed to increase diversity among educators, recognizing that representation affects curriculum content, pedagogical approaches, mentoring relationships, and institutional priorities.

Educational efforts to address racism face significant challenges and controversies. Since 2021, numerous states have enacted legislation restricting how racism and related topics can be taught in schools, often using the term "critical race theory" to encompass a broad range of educational approaches to racial justice. These restrictions have created chilling effects on educators and led to removal of diverse books and curricular materials. Even without formal restrictions, educators addressing racism often face resistance from parents, administrators, or community members who view such teaching as divisive or inappropriate for educational settings.

Teacher preparation represents another challenge, as many educators report feeling unprepared to effectively address race and racism in their classrooms. Professional development on these topics varies widely in quality and often lacks sustained support for implementation. Additionally, the teaching profession remains predominantly white (approximately 80% of K-12 teachers) despite increasingly diverse student populations, creating potential gaps in cultural knowledge and lived experience with racism.

Despite these challenges, education remains essential to long-term efforts to dismantle systemic racism. By helping students understand the historical development and contemporary manifestations of racial inequality, develop critical thinking skills to analyze racial messages in media and society, build cross-cultural communication abilities, and cultivate commitment to equity principles, educational institutions can contribute to developing a generation better equipped to create more just systems. However, realizing this potential requires addressing the ways educational institutions themselves perpetuate racial hierarchy through segregation, unequal funding, and biased practices. Truly anti-racist education must transform the structures of schooling even as it changes what happens within classrooms.

Pathways to Dismantling Systemic Racism

Addressing systemic racism requires comprehensive approaches that target both specific manifestations of racial inequality and the broader structures that maintain it. While individual awareness and behavior change matter, dismantling deeply embedded systems of advantage and disadvantage demands institutional transformation and policy reform across multiple domains. The most promising pathways combine targeted interventions to address specific disparities with broader structural changes to create more equitable systems.

Policing and criminal justice reform represents one critical pathway. Promising approaches include revising use of force policies to emphasize de-escalation, implementing robust accountability mechanisms for officer misconduct, ending practices like stop-and-frisk that disproportionately target people of color, and developing alternative response models for mental health crises and other situations where armed police may not be necessary. More fundamental transformations involve reconsidering how public safety is conceptualized and resourced, with some communities redirecting portions of police budgets toward prevention-oriented services addressing root causes of crime.

Voting rights protection and expansion is essential to ensuring that communities of color have equal voice in democratic processes. Key reforms include restoring provisions of the Voting Rights Act undermined by *Shelby County v. Holder*, implementing automatic voter registration, expanding early and mail-in voting options, ending felony disenfranchisement, and creating independent redistricting commissions to prevent racial gerrymandering. These measures help ensure that the officials making decisions affecting communities of color are accountable to those communities.

Housing policy offers particularly powerful leverage points for addressing systemic racism because residential patterns affect so many other outcomes, from education to health to wealth accumulation. Promising approaches include strengthening enforcement of fair housing laws, implementing inclusionary zoning requirements for affordable units in new developments, providing first-time homebuyer assistance targeted to historically excluded communities, and investing in affordable housing in high-opportunity neighborhoods. More ambitious proposals include reparations programs that specifically address historical housing discrimination and its intergenerational consequences.

Educational equity requires addressing both resource disparities and barriers to opportunity. Reform pathways include revising school funding formulas to reduce inequities between wealthy and low-income districts, implementing culturally responsive curriculum and pedagogy, reforming disciplinary practices that disproportionately impact students of color, and creating stronger pathways from K-12 to higher education and careers. Addressing segregation through controlled choice programs, magnet schools, and regional integration initiatives can help ensure that educational resources and opportunities don't remain concentrated in predominantly white schools.

Policy Reform

Changing laws and regulations that produce or permit racial disparities

Institutional Transformation

Reforming organizational practices, cultures, and structures that perpetuate inequality

Community Empowerment

Building capacity of affected communities to advocate for their needs and interests

Individual Change

Developing awareness, knowledge, and skills to recognize and challenge racism

Economic opportunity and wealth-building pathways are crucial for addressing racial economic inequality. Approaches include strengthening enforcement of employment discrimination laws, implementing targeted economic development in historically disinvested communities, expanding access to capital for minority-owned businesses, and developing programs to build assets among historically disadvantaged groups. Broader structural reforms might include baby bonds (government-funded trust accounts for newborns that grow until adulthood, with larger amounts for lower-income children) or reparations programs that directly address the economic legacy of slavery and subsequent discrimination.

Healthcare equity pathways include expanding insurance coverage to reduce racial gaps in access, increasing diversity in healthcare professions, implementing anti-bias training for providers, investing in healthcare facilities in underserved communities, and addressing social determinants of health through housing, environmental, and economic policies. Community-based approaches that partner with trusted organizations in communities of color can help overcome historical mistrust of medical institutions while delivering culturally appropriate care.

Individual and collective action both play important roles in these transformation processes. Individuals can educate themselves about systemic racism, examine their own biases and behaviors, support minority-owned businesses, advocate for policy changes, and participate in community organizations working toward racial justice. Collectively, communities can build power through organizing, form coalitions across racial lines around shared interests, hold institutions accountable through monitoring and advocacy, and develop alternative models that demonstrate more equitable approaches.

Successful pathways to dismantling systemic racism typically share certain characteristics: they address both immediate manifestations of inequality and root causes; they combine universal policies that benefit all with targeted approaches that address specific barriers facing communities of color; they ensure that those most affected by racism have meaningful voice in developing solutions; and they recognize the interconnected nature of different systems perpetuating racial inequality. While complete transformation requires long-term commitment, specific reforms can create meaningful improvements in people's lives while building momentum toward more fundamental change.

Call-to-Action: 10 Steps Towards a More Just and Equitable Nation

The following steps offer suggestions for how individuals, whether harmed by systemic racism or enriched by it, can actively contribute to the movement toward an equitable America where race does not determine one's destiny or access to opportunities.

1. **Educate and Engage:**
    - Educate yourself and others about the history and contemporary impacts of systemic racism.
    - Engage in discussions that confront uncomfortable truths about race and privilege.
    - Attend forums, webinars, or events focused on racial justice to stay engaged with ongoing conversations and actions.
2. **Support Targeted Policy Changes**:
    - Advocate for and support policies that address specific manifestations of racial inequality (e.g., housing, education, employment, healthcare).
    - Join or support organizations that focus on policy reform aimed at dismantling racistem.
3. **Build Cross-Community Solidarity**:
    - Participate in coalitions or community initiatives that bring together diverse racial and ethnic groups to work towards common goals.
    - Listen to and uplift voices from communities affected by systemic racism to ensure strategies are inclusive and respectful of specific experiences.

4. **Embrace Accountability**:
     - Reflect on your own privileges and how they contribute to existing systems of inequality.
     - Accept personal responsibly for actions or inactions that fuel disorderliness or sabotage collaboration among willing partners.
     - Take action in your personal and professional life to contribute to the equitable distribution of resources and opportunities
5. **Push and Encourage Institutions**:
     - Push local governments, corporations, educational institutions, and nonprofit organizations to examine their policies for perpetuating inequality.
     - Encourage these entities to commit to transparency, accountability, and reforms that promote equity.
6. **Balance Urgency with Long-term Commitment**:
     - Identify immediate actions you can take to reduce harm in your community, such as addressing youth dissension, supporting local anti-racism initiatives or volunteering with organizations addressing racial justice.
     - Commit to long-term involvement in the fight for racial equity, understanding that systemic change takes sustained effort across all demographics and generations.
7. **Reimagine National Identity**:
     - Advocate for a redefinition of American greatness based on equity, dignity, and justice rather than dominance and power.
     - Participate in campaigns or movements that call for policies reflecting these values, such as comprehensive immigration reform, equitable healthcare access, and fair labor practices.

8. **Share Knowledge and Resources:**
    - Use social media or local platforms to disseminate information and raise awareness about systemic racism and effective solutions.
    - Create or join book clubs, workshops, or discussion groups focused on racial equity and anti-racism.
9. **Understand the Reality and Impact of "Fatigue:"**
    - Offset the toll of constant vigilance and the concomitant psychological wear by embracing mental health diligences.
    - Shift the fatigue-plagued conversation around diversity, equity, and inclusion to highlight how a just society enriches everyone.
    - Resist the urge to succumb to inertia and exhaustion; instead, take action to unfreeze injustice and drive meaningful change.
10. **Encourage Others to Join:**
    - Inspire friends, family, and colleagues to participate in efforts addressing systemic racism by sharing your experiences and encouraging open dialogue.
    - Mobilize support for community events or educational opportunities that promote racial equity.

Historical perspective reminds us that previous generations faced even more daunting obstacles and nevertheless persevered to create meaningful change through persistent collective action. By building on this legacy while developing new approaches suited to contemporary challenges, we can continue the unfinished work of creating a nation where race no longer determines destiny and all people have genuine access to life, liberty, and the pursuit of happiness.

Glossary

Access Disparities: Inequities that affect different racial and ethnic groups in their ability to enroll in institutions of higher education.

Accountability Mechanisms: Systems or processes established to hold individuals or institutions responsible for their behavior or decisions, especially regarding misconduct.

Achievement Gaps: Discrepancies in academic performance and educational attainment between different groups, often defined by race or socioeconomic status, that emerge early in childhood and persist throughout education.

Affirmative Action: Policies that consider factors like race or gender in admission processes to promote diversity and counteract historical inequalities.

AIMM (Alliance for Inclusive and Multicultural Marketing): An initiative that aims to measure cultural relevance in advertising and promote inclusivity.

Algorithmic Bias: Disproportionate impacts of automated decision-making tools based on racial or gender categories, leading to inequitable treatment in areas like healthcare and law enforcement.

Algorithmic Discrimination: Instances where algorithm-driven processes (such as ad placements or job listings) lead to biased outcomes against certain demographic groups.

Alien Land Laws: Laws that prohibited "aliens" (particularly Asian immigrants) from owning land or property, reflecting systemic racial discrimination.

American Exceptionalism: The belief that the United States is inherently different from other nations, often characterized by a sense of superiority and a unique role in promoting democracy and freedom. This ideology has been intertwined with racial superiority narratives.

Bamboo Ceiling: The barriers Asian Americans face in advancing to leadership positions in workplaces despite high levels of education and representation.

Banking Deserts: Areas where residents have limited access to banking services due to the absence of bank branches or institutions.

Barriers to Opportunity: Obstacles that prevent certain groups from accessing resources, education, employment, and other opportunities necessary for advancement.

Bias and Cultural Competence Training: Programs intended to educate employees about implicit biases and develop skills to interact effectively with diverse populations, thereby promoting an inclusive workplace.

BIPOC: An acronym referring to Black, Indigenous, and People of Color; it emphasizes the unique experiences and challenges faced by these communities.

Boomerang Effect: The phenomenon where practices or policies originating from military actions abroad impact civilian life domestically, illustrating the interconnectedness of domestic and international systems of racism and violence.

Black Lives Matter (BLM): A decentralized political and social movement advocating for the rights and dignity of Black individuals and communities, addressing issues such as police violence, systemic racism, and social justice.

Brown v. Board of Education (1954): A landmark Supreme Court case that declared state laws establishing separate public schools for Black and white students unconstitutional, effectively ending legal school segregation.

Business Case for Diversity: The argument that diverse workforces can lead to competitive advantages for companies, such as enhanced creativity, improved decision-making, and better market insights.

Chinese Exclusion Act: A U.S. federal law enacted in 1882 that prohibited Chinese laborers from immigrating to the United States, reflecting racial discrimination in immigration policy.

Civic Engagement: Participation in political and social processes, including voting and community organizing, which can be hindered by systemic barriers in various racial communities.

Civil Rights Act of 1964: A significant piece of legislation that outlawed discrimination based on race, color, religion, sex, or national origin, prohibiting discrimination in public accommodations, employment, and federally funded programs.

Civil Rights Movement: A social movement in the United States aimed at ending racial segregation and discrimination against African Americans, particularly during the 1950s and 1960s, culminating in important legal reforms.

Collective Healing: Practices within a community aimed at recovering from trauma and strengthening resilience against oppression.

Colonial Power Dynamics: Economic and political relationships where dominant (often Western) countries exploit resources and labor in less powerful nations, typically former colonies. Such dynamics often maintain inequalities long after formal colonialism has ended

Colorblind Ideology: An ideological stance that emphasizes individual merit without recognizing how race influences opportunities, effectively preserving existing advantages.

Colorism: Discrimination based on skin tone, where lighter skin is favored over darker skin within the same racial or ethnic group, often reinforcing social hierarchies rooted in white nationalism.

Community Empowerment: Initiatives aimed at strengthening the ability of communities, particularly marginalized ones, to advocate for their rights and interests.

Community Reinvestment Act (CRA): A law designed to encourage banks to meet the needs of borrowers in all segments of the communities in which they operate, especially low- and moderate-income neighborhoods.

Comprehensive Approaches: Strategies that involve multiple strategies across different areas to tackle racism and promote equity rather than addressing issues in isolation.

Conditional Citizenship: The situation in which military service or loyalty grants marginalized groups limited recognition or rights, rather than full citizenship.

Creative Resistance: Artistic expressions and movements that push back against oppressive systems and narratives, often emerging from marginalized communities.

Criminal Justice Disparities: Racial imbalances witnessed in the criminal justice system, affecting policing, sentencing, and incarceration rates disproportionately among communities of color.

Critical Race Theory (CRT): An academic framework that examines how systemic racism is embedded in legal systems and policies, often scrutinized and debated in the context of educational curricula.

Cultural Appropriation: The adoption of elements from one culture by members of another culture, often without permission or understanding, which can reinforce power imbalances.

Cultural Erasure: The process by which a dominant culture suppresses or eliminates another culture through various means, including assimilation and oppression.

Cultural Genocide: Efforts to eliminate the cultural identity of a particular group, often involving the suppression of language, tradition, and history.

Cultural Norms: Shared beliefs and practices within a society that rationalize or reinforce existing hierarchies, including those based on race.

Culturally Competent Healthcare: Medical care that is respectful of and tailored to the cultural needs of patients from diverse backgrounds.

Data Gaps: Areas where insufficient data inhibit comprehensive understanding of racial inequalities, leading to challenges in addressing those disparities.

De-escalation: Strategies aimed at reducing tension or conflict in potentially volatile situations, particularly in law enforcement contexts.

DEI (Diversity, Equity, and Inclusion): A set of initiatives and practices within organizations aimed at promoting diversity among employees, ensuring equitable treatment and opportunities, and creating an inclusive workplace culture.

DEI Fatigue: A term used to describe the weariness or backlash against ongoing diversity, equity, and inclusion initiatives, often arising from perceived ineffectiveness or overemphasis on these topics.

Demilitarization of Police: Efforts to reduce the militarization of police departments and draw parallels between military operations and domestic law enforcement, emphasizing how both systems perpetuate inequality and oppression.

Digital Divide: The gap between individuals who have access to modern information and communication technology and those who do not, often reflecting socioeconomic disparities.

Digital Redlining: The practice of using algorithms and online marketing to segregate or limit access to certain groups based on demographic characteristics, reinforcing existing inequalities.

Disaggregation: The process of breaking down broad racial categories into more specific subcategories to better understand differences among them.

Discipline Disparities: Differences in disciplinary actions (such as suspensions) among students of different races, with disproportionate higher rates of punishment faced by students of color compared to their white peers.

Discrimination: Unjust or prejudicial treatment of different categories of people, particularly based on race or ethnicity.

Discriminatory Lending Practices: Unequal treatment in lending processes, resulting in higher rejection rates or unfavorable terms for borrowers based on race.

Disenfranchisement: The systematic stripping away of individuals' rights to vote or participate in democratic processes, often targeting specific racial or marginalized groups.

Disparate Impact Theory: A legal doctrine used to demonstrate that a policy is discriminatory if it disproportionately affects a particular racial group, regardless of intent.

Disparities in Media Investment: Unequal allocation of advertising spending among different demographic groups, particularly favoring white audiences over those of color.

Diversity in Healthcare Professions: Inclusion of individuals from various racial, ethnic, and cultural backgrounds within healthcare roles, which can enhance understanding and treatment of diverse populations.

Domestic Terrorism: Violent acts committed by individuals or groups within a country to promote ideological goals, especially when motivated by racial, social, or political beliefs.

Double V Campaign: A World War II-era campaign that urged African Americans to fight for victory against fascism abroad and for civil rights at home, highlighting the contradiction between fighting for freedom while facing racial segregation.

Economic Mobility: The ability of individuals or families to move up or down in socioeconomic status through income or wealth changes.

Economic Opportunity and Wealth-Building Pathways: Strategies aimed at improving economic outcomes and reducing wealth disparities for marginalized groups.

Economic Security: A state where individuals and families have stable financial resources to meet basic needs and withstand unexpected costs.

Economic Sovereignty: The capacity of a nation to control its economic policies and decisions without external interference or conditions imposed by foreign powers or institutions.

Educational Barriers: Obstacles that prevent equitable access to quality education, such as funding disparities or cultural disconnects between home and school environments.

Educational Equity: Ensuring equal access to education and educational resources regardless of race or socioeconomic status.

Employee Resource Groups (ERGs): Voluntary, employee-led groups formed around shared characteristics or life experiences, often fostering inclusivity and providing support and networking opportunities.

Employment Discrimination Laws: Regulations prohibiting unfair treatment of employees based on race, gender, ethnicity, and other characteristics.

Environmental Injustice: Disproportionate exposure of marginalized communities to environmental hazards, often due to systemic racism in policy and governance.

Environmental Justice Movement: A socio-political movement that advocates for fair treatment and involvement of all people, regardless of race or economic status, in environmental decisions affecting them.

Environmental Racism: The idea that minority groups are disproportionately exposed to environmental hazards and have less access to environmental benefits.

Epigenetics: The study of changes in gene expression that do not involve alterations to the underlying DNA sequence; research suggests extreme stress can lead to epigenetic changes that may affect subsequent generations.

Equal Employment Opportunity (EEO): Legal guidelines established to prohibit discrimination in hiring and employment practices based on characteristics such as race, gender, age, disability, and more.

Equitable Systems: Structures and practices designed to ensure fair treatment, access, opportunity, and advancement for all individuals, irrespective of their background.

Equity Audits: Regular assessments of organizational policies and practices to identify and address inequities, ensuring alignment with DEI goals.

Equity vs. Equality: Equity refers to fairness and justice in distribution of resources and opportunities, recognizing differing needs and historical disadvantages, while equality means providing the same resources or opportunities to all, regardless of need.

Ethnic Discount: A pricing bias where advertisers pay significantly less for ad placements targeting minority audiences compared to similar sized white audiences.

Exclusionary Citizenship: Laws that restrict citizenship rights based on race or ethnicity, preventing non-white immigrants from gaining the same status as white citizens.

Exclusionary Media Planning: The practice of deliberately excluding certain media outlets from advertising campaigns based on stereotypes regarding their audience's socioeconomic status or other unfounded assumptions.

Fair Housing Act (1968): A U.S. law that prohibits discrimination in housing based on race, color, national origin, religion, sex, familial status, or disability.

Faith-Based Resistance to Racism: Efforts within religious contexts and institutions to oppose racial injustices and promote equality, often motivated by theological principles of justice and human dignity.

Feedback Loops: Causal chains where initial disadvantages lead to further disadvantages over time, reinforcing existing inequities.

Felony Disenfranchisement: Laws that restrict voting rights for individuals with felony convictions, disproportionately affecting people of color.

Fence-line Communities: Neighborhoods that are in close proximity to industrial facilities, often bearing the brunt of pollution and its associated health effects.

Formal Equality: Legal frameworks that prohibit explicit discrimination but do not address structural barriers or rectify past injustices.

Gentrification: The process of transforming urban neighborhoods by attracting wealthier residents, often displacing lower-income residents and altering the character of the community.

Gerrymandering: The manipulation of electoral district boundaries to favor one party over another, often diluting the impact of votes from particular demographics.

Glass Ceiling: An invisible barrier preventing women and minorities from advancing in corporate hierarchies.

Global South: A term used to describe developing countries primarily located in Africa, Latin America, Asia, and Oceania. It is often contrasted with the "Global North," consisting of more economically developed nations.

Grandfather Clauses: Laws that allowed individuals to bypass literacy tests and poll taxes if their grandfathers had been eligible to vote before the Civil War, effectively excluding many Black voters.

Grassroots Activism: Collective action from the local level aiming to effect change, often characterized by community organizing and mobilization rather than relying on government or elite initiatives.

Group Black: An initiative providing economic empowerment to Black-owned media through targeted advertising spend.

Healthcare Equity: Efforts focused on ensuring that individuals have equitable access to healthcare services, irrespective of race or socioeconomic background.

Historic Marginalization: The long-standing and systemic exclusion of specific groups from social, economic, and political power.

Historical Roots: Refers to the origins and development of systemic racism, tracing back to colonial times, chattel slavery, the Constitution, and subsequent legal frameworks that have perpetuated racial inequality.

Historical Trauma: Collective emotional and psychological wounds resulting from significant historical events of oppression and violence, such as slavery and genocide.

Holistic Admissions Processes: Admissions criteria that consider a range of factors beyond standardized test scores, such as personal circumstances and achievements, to provide a more comprehensive view of applicants.

Housing Policy: Regulations and programs designed to address housing access, affordability, and discrimination; critical for addressing systemic inequalities.

Implicit Bias: Attitudes or stereotypes that affect understanding, actions, and decisions in an unconscious manner, often impacting clinical practices in healthcare.

Indigenous Activists: Members of Native American communities engaged in activism, focusing on the intersections of militarism, resource extraction, and colonialism, particularly concerning land rights and sovereignty.

Individual Racism: Personal prejudice, bias, or discrimination based on race, often manifested through explicit animus, conscious stereotyping, and unconscious bias in individual interactions.

Institutional Inertia: The tendency of established institutions to resist change and maintain existing norms or structures, leading to the perpetuation of racial inequalities even when attitudes may shift or the absence of conscious discrimination.

Institutional Racism: Racism that occurs within specific organizations and institutions, reflected in policies, practices, and procedures that disproportionately disadvantage certain racial groups.

Institutional Resistance: The opposition faced by policies aimed at equity reform from individuals or organizations benefiting from the status quo.

Institutional Transformation: Comprehensive changes within organizations to reform practices, cultures, and structures that perpetuate racial inequality.

Intergenerational Trauma: Trauma transmitted from one generation to another, often observed in communities historically subjected to oppression, affecting psychological and social wellbeing across generations.

Intergenerational Wealth Transfer: The passing down of financial resources, assets, or social advantages from parents to offspring, which can reinforce racial inequalities over generations.

Internalized Oppression: A phenomenon where individuals and communities adopt and perpetuate oppressive hierarchical beliefs about skin tone, affecting how they view themselves and others.

Internalized Racism: When individuals accept negative stereotypes and beliefs about their racial group, leading to diminished self-worth and perpetuation of societal biases.

Intersectionality: A framework developed by Kimberlé Crenshaw recognizing the overlap of multiple identities (such as race, gender, and class) and how they contribute to unique experiences of discrimination or privilege.

Jim Crow Laws: State and local statutes enacted in the southern United States enforcing racial segregation and disenfranchising Black Americans post-Civil War.

K-12 Educational Inequities: Disparities in the quality and resources provided by primary and secondary school systems across different neighborhoods and regions.

Keyword Exclusion Lists: Lists used to prevent ads from appearing alongside certain topics, often blocking discussions around sensitive issues such as racism.

Legacy Admissions: College admission policies that favor applicants with family connections to alumni, which often advantages white students due to historical exclusions faced by students of color.

Legal Frameworks: Laws and regulations that govern societal behavior and institutional practices, which can either uphold or challenge systemic racism.

Literacy Tests: Evaluations requiring individuals to demonstrate reading comprehension as a prerequisite for voting, often applied unfairly against minority communities.

LULUs (Locally Unwanted Land Uses): Facilities or developments that are detrimental to a local area, including landfills, incinerators, and other sources of pollution.

Mass Incarceration: A significant increase in incarceration rates in the United States, particularly affecting communities of color due to policy choices rather than crime rates.

Measurement and Data Bias: The tendency of audience measurement systems to inaccurately count or represent minority groups, leading to unjustified advertising decisions.

Mental Health Crises Response Models: Alternate frameworks for addressing mental health emergencies that do not involve armed police, focusing instead on trained mental health professionals.

Meritocracy Myth: The belief that success is primarily a result of individual effort and ability, which ignores structural barriers faced by marginalized groups.

Microaggressions: Subtle, everyday interactions or behaviors that convey prejudiced attitudes towards a marginalized group, often unconsciously.

Minority Business Enterprises (MBEs): Companies that are at least 51% owned and operated by individuals from minority groups.

Model Minority Stereotype: A concept that portrays certain minority groups, particularly Asian Americans, as successful and industrious, which can create unrealistic expectations and obscure the challenges faced by individuals within those communities.

"Muslim Ban": A policy implemented by the Trump administration restricting travel and immigration from several predominantly Muslim countries. It exemplifies how immigration policies can reflect racial and religious biases.

National Identity and Purpose: The collective values, beliefs, and ideals that define a nation and guide its actions; reimagining these in the context of equity involves focusing on dignity and justice for all.

News Media Representation: The portrayal of racial and ethnic groups in news stories, significantly impacting public perceptions and social attitudes.

NIMBY (Not In My Back Yard): A phenomenon where residents oppose the siting of undesirable facilities (such as waste sites) near their own community but may not oppose them being located in others' neighborhoods.

Organizational Culture: The shared values, beliefs, and practices within an organization that can harbor systemic biases affecting decision-making processes.

Pay Equity Analysis: The evaluation of compensation structures to ensure fair pay across different demographics, addressing potential disparities.

Pedagogy (Culturally Responsive): An educational approach that recognizes and incorporates students' cultural backgrounds and experiences into the teaching process, aiming to engage and empower all learners.

Perpetual Foreigner Stereotype: A stereotype that assumes individuals of certain racial or ethnic backgrounds (especially Asian Americans) are not native citizens regardless of their actual citizenship status.

Plessy v. Ferguson (1896): Supreme Court decision that established the "separate but equal" doctrine, providing constitutional justification for legalized segregation.

Poll Taxes: Fees required to be paid in order to vote, historically used to disenfranchise poorer citizens, particularly African Americans.

Public Health Emergency: A situation characterized by a significant threat to the health of a population, requiring coordinated efforts for effective management.

Race-Neutral Policies: Policies that do not explicitly consider race but may lead to disparate impacts across different racial groups due to existing structural inequalities.

Racial Battle Fatigue: The cumulative psychological toll experienced by individuals of color due to ongoing experiences of racism, discrimination, and vigilance in predominantly white spaces.

Racial Equity Work: Efforts undertaken to create fair treatment, access, opportunity, and advancement for all individuals, while striving to identify and eliminate barriers that have historically led to unequal treatment based on race.

Racial Hierarchy: A social system in which different races are assigned varying degrees of privilege and power, typically privileging white individuals over people of color.

Racial Socialization: The process by which parents and families prepare children to navigate a racially stratified society, promoting positive cultural identity while also preparing them for societal discrimination.

Racial Trauma: Psychological harm experienced due to cumulative racial discrimination and prejudice, often exhibiting symptoms similar to post-traumatic stress disorder.

Racial Wealth Gap: The disparity in asset ownership between different racial groups, often resulting from historical injustices and compounded economic barriers.

Racialized Enemies: The portrayal of enemy combatants through a lens of racial stereotypes in wartime propaganda, which fosters dehumanization and reinforces domestic racism against certain ethnic groups.

Racialization of National Identity: The construction of national identity that privileges whiteness, often defining citizenship and belonging through racial terms, marginalizing non-white individuals.

Racistem: A portmanteau of "racism" and "system," it describes how racial discrimination is embedded within the fabric of American society, affecting individuals at multiple levels.

Redistricting Commissions: Independent bodies that draw electoral district boundaries to prevent gerrymandering, which can dilute minority voting power.

Redlining: The practice of denying or limiting mortgages and insurance to communities based on racial composition, often resulting in long-term economic disadvantages for these areas.

Regents of the University of California v. Bakke (1978): A Supreme Court decision that placed significant constraints on affirmative action in higher education.

Regulatory Barriers: Rules and regulations that disproportionately affect certain groups, hindering their ability to succeed in business or access services.

Reinforcing Systems: Feedback loops where disadvantages in one area (e.g., housing segregation) lead to further disadvantages in other areas (e.g., educational opportunities), perpetuating cycles of inequality.

Reparations: Compensation intended to make amends for historical injustices, particularly those related to slavery and systemic discrimination.

Resource Extraction: The process of removing natural resources from the environment, which can lead to environmental degradation and disproportionately affect marginalized communities.

Resume Audit Studies: Research methods used to analyze discrimination in hiring, typically by submitting identical resumes under different racial identities.

Ruby Bridges: An American civil rights activist who gained national attention at the age of six when she was the first African American child to integrate an all-white elementary school in New Orleans, Louisiana, in 1960.

School-to-Prison Pipeline: A term describing how punitive school policies, primarily affecting students of color, increase the likelihood of involvement with the criminal justice system.

Secular Perception: The perspective by which certain stereotypes about racial groups are accepted as normative, contributing to social divisions and discrimination.

Selectivity in Higher Education: The criteria and standards used by colleges and universities to admit students, often favoring those with more resources and achievements.

Shelby County v. Holder (2013): A Supreme Court decision that invalidated key provisions of the Voting Rights Act, enabling states to enact voting laws without federal approval, which led to new restrictions affecting minority voters.

Social Capital: The networks of relationships among people who live and work in a particular society, enabling individuals to gain access to resources and information.

Social Determinants of Health: Conditions such as economic stability, education, and social and community context that affect an individual's health outcomes.

Social Mobility: The ability of individuals or families to move up or down the socio-economic ladder, which can be affected by access to education and opportunities.

Socioeconomic Status: An individual's or group's economic and social position in relation to others, often based on income, education, and occupation.

Sovereignty: The authority of a state or governing body to govern itself or another state, often referenced concerning tribal nations' rights.

STEMM Fields: An acronym referring to science, technology, engineering, mathematics, and medicine, domains often perceived as meritocratic yet influenced by systemic racism.

Stereotype Threat: The fear or anxiety that individuals may experience when they perceive that they might confirm negative stereotypes associated with their racial or ethnic group, detrimentally affecting their performance.

Stop-and-Frisk: A police practice allowing officers to stop, question, and search individuals for weapons or contraband, often criticized for its disproportionate impact on people of color.

Structural Racism: The overarching system of interconnected institutions and cultural narratives that create and maintain racial inequalities across society, encompassing both past and present inequities.

Structural Reforms: Broad changes in policies, institutions, or practices that aim to redistribute power and resources more equitably across society.

Students for Fair Admissions v. Harvard (2023): A Supreme Court decision that effectively prohibited race-conscious admissions policies in higher education,

Systemic Racism: A complex network of embedded policies, practices, and cultural norms that collectively disadvantage racial and ethnic minority groups while preserving privileges for the dominant group.

Targeted Interventions: Specific actions aimed at addressing particular issues or disparities faced by marginalized communities.

The GI Bill: Legislation providing benefits to World War II veterans, which disproportionately excluded Black veterans from accessing education and housing benefits.

The Great Migration: The mass movement of millions of Black Americans from the rural South to Northern and Western urban centers during the 20th century, seeking better opportunities but often facing new forms of discrimination.

Three-Fifths Compromise: A constitutional agreement made in 1787 that counted three-fifths of the enslaved population for purposes of taxation and representation in Congress, highlighting institutionalized racism.

Title VI Complaints: Refers to complaints made under Title VI of the Civil Rights Act, which prohibits discrimination on the basis of race, color, or national origin in programs receiving federal financial assistance.

Tokenism: The practice of including a minimal number of people from marginalized groups in positions of influence to give an illusion of diversity, without meaningful involvement or impact.

Tracking Systems: Educational practices that place students in different academic levels based on perceived ability, often disadvantaging students of color.

Tuskegee Syphilis Study: An infamous study where untreated syphilis was allowed to progress in Black men under the guise of medical research, resulting in a legacy of mistrust in the healthcare system.

Tulsa Race Massacre: One of the most violent racial conflict events in U.S. history which took place in the Greenwood District of Tulsa, Oklahoma, a prosperous African American community known as "Black Wall Street."

Unequal Burdens and Opportunities: The concept that marginalized communities are disproportionately impacted by the burdens of military service, facing higher risks in combat while receiving fewer benefits compared to other groups.

Unconscious Bias: Implicit judgments and stereotypes that affect decision-making and behavior unconsciously, often reflecting societal prejudices.

Under-resourced Schools: Educational institutions that lack adequate funding, qualified staff, and necessary facilities, disproportionately affecting marginalized student populations.

Use of Force Policies: Regulations governing how police officers may use force, emphasizing de-escalation techniques to minimize violent interactions.

Vaccine Hesitancy: Delay in acceptance or refusal of vaccines despite availability, influenced by trust issues stemming from historic injustices or misinformation.

Voter Suppression: Tactics used to discourage or prevent specific groups of people from voting.

Voting Rights Act of 1965: Legislation designed to eliminate various barriers to voting for African Americans, including literacy tests and other discriminatory practices, and established federal oversight of election processes in areas with histories of discrimination.

Voting Rights Protection and Expansion: Measures to ensure equal access to voting for all citizens, particularly marginalized communities.

Vulnerability to Climate Change: Increased susceptibility of certain communities—often those marginalized racially or economically—to the adverse impacts of climate change.

Wealth Accumulation: The process by which an individual or community builds wealth over time through assets, investments, and savings.

Weathering: A phenomenon where chronic stress from systemic racism leads to faster aging and increased vulnerabilities to health problems.

Resources and References

Historical Roots of Systemic Racism
- Davis, Angela Y. *Women, Race, & Class*. New York: Vintage Books, 1983.
- Du Bois, W.E.B. *The Souls of Black Folk*. Chicago: A.C. McClurg & Co., 1903.
- Omi, Michael, and Howard Winant. *Racial Formation in the United States*. 3rd ed. New York: Routledge, 2014.

Contemporary Manifestations of Systemic Racism
- Kendi, Ibram X. *How to Be an Antiracist*. New York: One World, 2019.
- Alexander, Michelle. *The New Jim Crow: Mass Incarceration in the Age of Colorblindness*. New York: The New Press, 2010.
- Pager, Devah. "The Mark of a Criminal Record." *American Journal of Sociology* 108, no. 5 (2003): 937-975.

Pathways Toward Dismantling Systems of Inequality
- Crenshaw, Kimberlé. "Mapping the Margins: Intersectionality, Identity Politics, and Violence against Women of Color." *Stanford Law Review* 43, no. 6 (1991): 1241-1299.
- The Sentencing Project. *Report on Racial Disparities in Criminal Justice*. Accessed October 2023.
- United Nations Human Rights Council. "Promoting Reconciliation, Accountability and Human Rights in Sri Lanka." A/HRC/22/38, 2013.

Understanding Different Manifestations of Racism
- Tatum, Beverly Daniel. *Why Are All the Black Kids Sitting Together in the Cafeteria? And Other Conversations About Race*. New York: Basic Books, 2017.
- Ridolfo, Chris. "Breaking Down Institutional Racism: Moving Beyond Individual Biases." *Harvard Political Review*, September 14, 2020.
- Stevenson, Bryan. *Just Mercy: A Story of Justice and Redemption*. New York: Spiegel & Grau, 2014.

Foundational Texts on Structural Racism
- Williams, D. R., and S. A. Mohammed. "Discrimination and Racial Disparities in Health: Evidence and Needed Research." *Journal of Behavioral Medicine* 32, no. 1 (2009): 20-47.
- Alexander, Michelle. *The New Jim Crow: Mass Incarceration in the Age of Colorblindness*. New York: The New Press, 2010.
- Crenshaw, Kimberlé. "Mapping the Margins: Intersectionality, Identity Politics, and Violence against Women of Color." *Stanford Law Review* 43, no. 6 (1991): 1241-1299.

Legal Frameworks and Historical Context
- Sugrue, Thomas J. *The Origins of the Urban Crisis: Race and Inequality in Postwar Detroit*. Princeton University Press, 1996.
- Rothstein, Richard. *The Color of Law: A Forgotten History of How Our Government Segregated America*. Liveright Publishing Corporation, 2017.

Education and Institutional Racism
- Ladson-Billings, Gloria. "From the Achievement Gap to the Education Debt: Understanding Achievement in U.S. Schools." *Educational Researcher* 35, no. 7 (2006): 3-12.
- Orfield, Gary, and Chungmei Lee. *Racial Transformation and the Changing Nature of Segregation*. Harvard Civil Rights Project, 2006.

The Role of Public Policy
- Massey, Douglas S., and Nancy A. Denton. *American Apartheid: Segregation and the Making of the Underclass*. Harvard University Press, 1993.
- Ayres, Ian. *Super Crunchers: Why Thinking-By-Numbers Is the New Way to Be Right*. Bantam Books, 2007.

Foreign Policy
- Anderson, M. (2020). Racial Hierarchies in U.S. Foreign Policy: A Historical Perspective. Journal of International Relations, 25(3), 45-67.
- Jones, T. (2018). American Exceptionalism and Racial Superiority: The Justification for Interventionism. Global Studies Quarterly, 12(4), 100-121.
- Lee, K. (2019). The Impact of Immigration Policies on Racial Dynamics in the United States. Social Policy Review, 14(2), 78-95.
- Smith, J. (2021). Colonial Legacies in Trade Agreements: The Reproduction of Power Dynamics. Economic Development Journal, 33(1), 22-42.
- Roberts, L. & Perez, D. (2022). Structural Adjustment Programs and Their Disproportionate Effects on Non-White Nations. Development Studies Quarterly, 15(3), 55-79.
- Thompson, R. (2017). The Devaluation of Non-White Lives in Military Interventions: A Critical Analysis. Conflict and Society, 9(2), 134-150.
- White, E. & Johnson, A. (2023). Policy Intention vs. Racial Realities: Bridging the Gap for Equity in U.S. Foreign Policy. Journal of Race and Politics, 28(1), 10-30.

Domestic Terrorism
- Federal Bureau of Investigation (FBI). *A Summary of the Domestic Terrorism Threat*. FBI, 2020.
  - This overarching report from the FBI documents current threats from various domestic extremist groups, including white supremacists.
- Squires, Gregory D. *The Politics of Race and Crime: The Cause of Domestic Terrorism*. Critical Sociology, vol. 44, no. 1, 2018, pp. 261-275.
  - Discusses the racial underpinnings of domestic terrorism and the government's response to it.
- Southern Poverty Law Center (SPLC). *The Year in Hate and Extremism 2020*. SPLC, 2020.
  - An annual report detailing the activities and trends of hate groups in the US, with specific emphasis on white supremacist violence.
- Dunbar-Ortiz, Roxanne. *An Indigenous Peoples' History of the United States*. Beacon Press, 2014.
  - Although focusing on Indigenous peoples historically, this book addresses broader patterns of violence and systemic racism against marginalized groups.
- Beeson, Jillian. *Racialized Violence and the Limits of Civil Discourse*. Social Problems, vol. 67, no. 3, 2020, pp. 375-392.
  - This paper examines the societal implications of racialized violence, connecting hate crimes with social and political conflicts.

Contemporary Issues and Extending Discussions
- Zuberi, Tawanna, and Eduardo Bonilla-Silva. *White Logic, White Methods: Racism and Methodology*. Rowman & Littlefield Publishers, 2008.
- Kendi, Ibram X. *How to Be an Antiracist*. One World, 2019.

Reports and Data Sources
- U.S. Department of Education Office for Civil Rights. *Report to Congress on the Implementation of Title VI of the Civil Rights Act of 1964*. Washington, DC: U.S. Department of Education, 2020.

- Pew Research Center. "The Link Between Discrimination and Economic Disparities." Washington, DC: Pew Research Center, 2020. 26

Higher Education and Representation Issues
- U.S. Department of Education. (2021). *Digest of Education Statistics, 2020.* NCES 2021-009.
- Pew Research Center. (2021). *The State of College Enrollment & Completion.* Retrieved from https://www.pewresearch.org
- National Science Foundation. (2019). *Survey of Graduate Students and Postdoctorates in Science and Engineering.*

Housing and Redlining
- U.S. Department of Housing and Urban Development. (n.d.). *The Federal Housing Administration: A History.*
- Brookings Institution. (2021). *The enduring legacy of redlining.* Retrieved from https://www.brookings.edu
- Urban Institute. (n.d.). *The Impact of Redlining on Housing Affordability in Baltimore.*

Impact on Homeownership and Wealth
- U.S. Census Bureau. (2021). *Homeownership Rates by Race and Ethnicity.*
- Board of Governors of the Federal Reserve System. (2020). *Survey of Consumer Finances.*
- Brookings Institution. (2018). *How the Neighborhoods We Live In Affect Our Economic Status.*

Racism in Health Care
- U.S. Census Bureau. (2020). *Health Insurance Coverage in the United States: 2020.*
- Institute of Medicine. (2003). *Unequal Treatment: Confronting Racial and Ethnic Disparities in Health Care.*
- Ye, J., et al. (2020). *Maternal Mortality in the United States.* Centers for Disease Control and Prevention.

Criminal Justice System Bias
- Federal Bureau of Investigation. (2020). *Crime in the United States 2020.* Retrieved from https://www.fbi.gov
- U.S. Sentencing Commission. (2017). *Report on the Continuing Impact of the Fair Sentencing Act.*
- NAACP. (n.d.). *Criminal Justice Fact Sheet.*
- Pew Charitable Trusts. (n.d.). *Pretrial Detention's Impact on Convictions and Sentences.*

Voting Rights and Representation
- National Archives and Records Administration. (n.d.). *The Voting Rights Act of 1965: A Long Struggle for the Right to Vote.* Retrieved from [link]
- U.S. Department of Justice. (n.d.). *History of Voting Rights Act.* Retrieved from [link]
- Pew Research Center. (n.d.). *The Future of Voting: A Closer Look at Voter Trends in America.* Retrieved from [link]
- Voting Rights Project. (n.d.). *Shelby County v. Holder.* Retrieved from [link]

Employment and Workplace Discrimination
- U.S. Bureau of Labor Statistics. (n.d.). *Economic News Release: Labor Force Statistics from the Current Population Survey.* Retrieved from [link]
- Institute for Women's Policy Research. (n.d.). *Black Women's Employment in the United States.* Retrieved from [link]
- Dobbin, F., & Kalev, A. (n.d.). *Why Diversity Programs Fail.* Harvard Business Review. Retrieved from [link]

- Bertrand, M., & Mullainathan, S. (2004). *Are Emily and Greg More Employable than Lakisha and Jamal?* American Economic Review.

Economic Opportunity and Inequality
- Federal Reserve Board. (n.d.). *Distributional Financial Accounts of the United States*. Retrieved from [link]
- U.S. Census Bureau. (2020). *Income and Poverty in the United States: 2020*. Retrieved from [link]
- Chetty, R., et al. (n.d.). *The Opportunity Atlas*. Retrieved from [link]
- Brookings Institution. (n.d.). *The racial wealth gap: A new look at the gap between black and white families*. Retrieved from [link]

Business and Entrepreneurship
- U.S. Small Business Administration. (n.d.). *2020 Small Business Profiles for the States and Territories*. Retrieved from [link]
- Kauffman Foundation. (n.d.). *The Kauffman Index of Entrepreneurs*. Retrieved from [link]
- McKinsey & Company. (n.d.). *Diversity wins: How inclusion matters*. Retrieved from [link]
- Startup Genome. (2021). *The Global Startup Ecosystem Report 2021*. Retrieved from [link]

Access to Capital and Banking
- Federal Deposit Insurance Corporation. *2019 FDIC National Survey of Unbanked and Underbanked Households*. FDIC, 2019.
- National Community Reinvestment Coalition. *Gentrification in the District of Columbia*. National Community Reinvestment Coalition, 2020.
- Center for Responsible Lending. *Reports on Housing Discrimination and Lending Disparities*. Center for Responsible Lending, 2020.
- Economic Policy Institute. *The Racial Wealth Gap: A Key Barrier to Economic Mobility*. Economic Policy Institute, 2020.

Media and Cultural Representation
- Hall, Stuart. *Representation: Cultural Representations and Signifying Practices*. SAGE Publications, 1997.
- Dixon, Travis L., and María Elana D. McMahon. "Crime News and Racialized Beliefs: A Study of the Relationship Between Crime News Consumption and Racial Attitudes." *Journal of Broadcasting & Electronic Media*, vol. 58, no. 3, 2014, pp. 364-382.
- Gonzalez, L. "Understanding the Roles of Ethnic/Racial Minorities in Television Ads: A Double-Edged Sword?" *Journal of Advertising Research*, vol. 60, no. 3, 2020, pp. 291-303.
- Columbia Journalism Review. *Journalism's Diversity Problem*. Columbia Journalism Review, 2020.
- Smith, S. L., Choueiti, M., and Pieper, K. *Inequality in 1,200 Popular Films: Examining Race/Ethnicity and Gender of Characters Across 1,200 Films from 2007 to 2018*. Annenberg Inclusion Initiative, 2019.

The Music Industry
- George, Nelson. *The Death of Rhythm & Blues*. Penguin Press, 1988.
- Tischler, Barbara. "Racial Bias, Artistic Control, & Exploitation in the Music Industry." *Ethnomusicology*, vol. 64, no. 3, 2020, pp. 377-401.
- Cohen, Sara. *Decline, Renewal and the City in Popular Music Culture: Beyond the Beatles*. Cultural Studies, 1997.

Advertising and Media Buying
- American Association of Advertising Agencies. (2023). Equity & Inclusion Congress. Retrieved from https://www.aaaa.org/equity-inclusion

- Allred, N. (2021). The ethnic discount in advertising: Racial disparities in media buying. Journal of Marketing Research, 58(4), 733-747.
- Alliance for Inclusive and Multicultural Marketing. (2022). Cultural Insights Impact Measure. Retrieved from https://www.aimm.co/cultural-insights-impact-measure
- Bennett, S. E., & Gibbons, D. (2020). Digital advertising and algorithmic discrimination: Examining the impact on minority communities. Journal of Advertising, 49(2), 193-206.
- Group Black. (2023). Economic Empowerment offerings for minority-owned media. Retrieved from https://www.groupblack.com/economic-empowerment
- Johnson, M., & Roberts, L. (2021). Disparities in media investment: The case for change. International Journal of Business and Social Science, 12(5), 52-61.
- Nielsen. (2020). The State of Black Consumers 2020. Retrieved from https://www.nielsen.com/us/en/insights/report/2020/state-of-black-consumers/
- Peterson, R. A. (2021). Exclusionary practices in media planning: Challenging industry norms. Advertising Age, 92(3), 48-50.
- Smith, T., & Martinez, A. (2023). Reforming advertising practices: Current initiatives and their effectiveness. Journal of Advertising Research, 63(1), 15-25.
- Williams, K. (2022). Ownership disparities in advertising agencies: The need for systemic change. Journal of Marketing Diversity, 11(1), 32-45.

Psychological Impact of Systemic Racism
- Williams, David R., and Michelle Sternthal. "Understanding Racial/Ethnic Disparities in Health in Late Life: A Life-Course Perspective." *Journal of Health and Social Behavior*, vol. 51, no. 1_suppl, 2010, pp. S86-S101.
- Sue, Derald Wing. *Microaggressions in Everyday Life: Race, Gender, and Sexual Orientation*. Wiley, 2010.

Intersectionality
- Crenshaw, Kimberlé. "Mapping the Margins: Intersectionality, Identity Politics, and Violence Against Women of Color." *Stanford Law Review*, vol. 43, no. 6, 1991, pp. 1241-1299.
- Collins, Patricia Hill. *Black Feminist Thought: Knowledge, Consciousness, and the Politics of Empowerment*. Routledge, 2000.
- Agnew, Robert. "A Revised Strain Theory of Delinquency." *Social Forces*, vol. 70, no. 1, 1991, pp. 139-158.

Child and Youth Outcomes
- **Achievement Gaps**
  - Hart, B., & Risley, T. R. (1995). *Meaningful differences in the everyday experience of young American children*. Baltimore: Brookes Publishing.
  - Lee, J. & Burkham, D. T. (2002). *Inequality at the starting gate: Cognitive inequality among races and socioeconomic groups at the beginning of school*. Washington, DC: Economic Policy Institute.
- **Discipline Disparities**
  - U.S. Department of Education Office for Civil Rights. (2014). *Civil rights data collection: Data snapshot (school discipline)*.
  - Skiba, R. J., et al. (2011). *New directions in disciplinary policy and practice*. Social Policy Report.
- **Environmental Factors**

- - Paul, M., & Weller, C. (2016). *The costs of racism: Health consequences from environmental racism*. American Journal of Public Health.
  - Lanphear, B. P., et al. (2005). *Low-level lead exposure and children's IQ: A meta-analysis and systematic review*. Environmental Health Perspectives.
- **Psychological Impacts**
  - Williams, D. R., & Mohammed, S. A. (2009). *Discrimination and racial disparities in health: Evidence and needed research*. Journal of Behavioral Medicine.
  - Carter, R. T. (2007). *Racism and psychological and emotional injury: Recognizing and assessing race-based trauma*.
- **Weathering**
  - Geronimus, A. T. (1996). *Black/white differences in birth outcomes: The social context of maternal age*. Ethnicity & Disease.

Intergenerational Trauma
- **Historical Trauma**
  - Brave Heart, M. Y. H. (1998). *The historical trauma response among Natives and its relationship with substance abuse: A Lakota illustration*. Journal of Psychoactive Drugs.
  - Duran, E. (2006). *Healing the soul wound: Counseling with American Indians and other Native peoples*. Albuquerque: University of New Mexico Press.
- **Transgenerational Effects**
  - Yehuda, R., et al. (2001). *Effects of trauma on memory and cognition in Holocaust survivors: A critical review*. Cognitive Neuropsychiatry.

Colorism
- Hannahan, Jennifer. (2018). *Colorism: A New Perspective*. Oxford University Press.
  o This book provides a comprehensive overview of colorism, exploring its historical roots and contemporary implications.
- Hunter, Mae N. (2007). *Race, Gender, and the Politics of Skin Tone*. Routledge.
  o Hunter delves into how skin tone affects social status and opportunities within Black communities, providing valuable insights into internalized racism and discrimination.
- Telles, Edward E., & Lim, Suehoney S. (2002). "Racial Ambivalence and the American Dream: Skin Color and Income in Brazil and the United States." *Ethnic and Racial Studies*, 25(5), 853-874.
  o This study compares the impact of skin color on income in the U.S. and Brazil, illustrating the global implications of colorism.
- Byers, Darnell L. (2010). "The Impact of Colorism on African American Women's Life Experiences." *Journal of Black Studies*, 40(4), 725–741.
  o This article discusses how colorism specifically impacts the experiences of African American women, addressing intersectionality with gender.
- Russell, Kathy, Wilson, Midge, & Hall, Ronald. (1993). *The Color Complex: The Politics of Skin Color Among African Americans*. HarperCollins.

Role of Religion and Faith Institutions
- McDaniel, K. M. (2020). *Faith and force: An introduction to the history of religion and violence in America*. In A. M. Clemmons (Ed.), *The Wiley Blackwell companion to religion and violence*.

- Clemmons, A. M. (2014). *Religion and the politics of suffering*. Journal of Church and State.
- McRoberts, O. (2003). *Race, religion, and resistance in the black community*.
- Dantley, M. E. (2005). *The role of spirituality in educational leadership*. International Journal of Leadership in Education.

Racialization of National Identity
- Takaki, R. (1993). *A different mirror: A history of multicultural America*. Boston: Little, Brown and Company.
- Zinn, H. (1999). *A people's history of the United States*. New York: Harper Perennial.
- Ajrouch, K. J., & Jamal, A. (2007). *Social networks among Arab Americans*. Journal of Ethnic and Migration Studies.

Institutional Racism in STEMM
- National Science Foundation. (2019). *Women, minorities, and ersons with disabilities in science and engineering*.
- Melguizo, T., et al. (2011). *The role of minority-serving institutions in increasing racial/ethnic diversity in STEM*. Research in Higher Education.
- Awan, M. A., et al. (2017). *Disparities in academic performance in science, technology, engineering, and mathematics (STEM) courses*.

Environmental Racism
- Bullard, R. D. (1993). *Confronting Environmental Racism: Voices from the Grassroots*. South End Press.
- U.S. Environmental Protection Agency (EPA). Office of Environmental Justice. Retrieved from EPA Website.
- Zhang, W., & McCright, A. M. (2021). *Racial disparities in exposure to air pollution: Evidence from the United States*. Environmental Science & Technology Letters, 8(10), 811-817. https://doi.org/10.1021/acs.estlett.1c00738
- Saha, R., & Mohai, P. (2019). *Environmental injustice in the USA: The effects of race and class on exposure to environmental hazards*. Environmental Science & Policy, 101, 173-179. https://doi.org/10.1016/j.envsci.2019.08.005
- M. J. S. B., et al. (2020). *The Fisherman's Daughter: COVID-19 Exacerbates Environmental Justice Inequities*. Environmental Research Letters, 15(8), 084015.

Systemic Racism Against Native Americans
- Wilkins, D. E., & Stark, H. (2017). *American Indian Politics and the American Political System*. Rowman & Littlefield Publishers.
- National Congress of American Indians (NCAI). Reports on issues like funding for healthcare and education for Native American populations. Retrieved from NCAI Website.
- Indian Health Service (IHS) statistics: Healthcare inequities and underfunding data. Retrieved from IHS Website.
- Department of Justice (DOJ). Report on violence against Native women.
- King, R. J. (2019). *The Indian Removal Act: Four Treaties*. U.S. National Park Service.

Systemic Racism Affecting Latino Communities
- Pew Research Center. (2020). *Statistical Portrait of Hispanics in the United States*. Retrieved from Pew Research.
- National Council of La Raza. Issues and challenges faced by Latino families. Retrieved from NCLR Website.
- Florida State University study. Audit studies show discrimination patterns related to inflated housing costs.

- U.S. Census Bureau. Data on poverty, income levels, and community demographics.
- Cáceres, L., & Ponterotto, J. G. (2018). *The Complex Nature of Hispanic Experiences with Immigrant Status and Other Forms of Socioeconomic Inequality*. Journal of Hispanic Higher Education.

Systemic Racism Affecting Asian Americans

- Lee, J., & Bean, F. D. (2010). *America's changing color lines: Immigration, Race/Ethnicity, and Multiraciality*. CSDE Working Paper; UW Center for Studies in Demography and Ecology.
- APIA Scholars. Various reports on the educational outcomes and economic experiences of Asian Americans. Retrieved from APIA Scholars Website.
- Jeung, R. K., et al. (2021). *AAPI Hate Incidents Report*. Stop AAPI Hate.
- Wong, J., et al. (2011). *The 'Model Minority' Myth and Its Implications for Asian Americans. Social Forces*, 89(4), 1505-1530.
- Crenshaw, K. (1991). *Mapping the Margins: Intersectionality, Identity Politics, and Violence against Women of Color. Stanford Law Review*.

General Resources

- Environmental Protection Agency (EPA). Environmental justice reports. Retrieved from EPA Website.
- Reports by Civil Rights Organizations: NAACP, ACLU regarding systemic racism and inequality.
- Scholarly Articles and Journals: Access powerful peer-reviewed literature through platforms like JSTOR, Google Scholar, or university databases.

Institutional Inertia and Systemic Racism

- Alexander, M. (2010). *The New Jim Crow: Mass Incarceration in the Age of Colorblindness*. The New Press. This book discusses how structural and institutional practices perpetuate racial inequality even when explicit legal discrimination has been abolished.
- Bonilla-Silva, E. (2014). *The Structure of Racism in Color-Blind Society. American Sociological Review*, 70(3), 629-652. This article critiques colorblind ideologies and their implication in maintaining systemic inequalities.

Educational Inequities

- Orfield, G., & Lee, C. (2005). *Why Segregation Matters: Poverty and Educational Inequality*. The Civil Rights Project, Harvard University. This report emphasizes how funding based on property taxes reinforces educational inequities along racial lines.
- Reardon, S. F. (2011). "The Widening Academic Achievement Gap Between the Rich and the Poor: New Evidence and Possible Explanations." *Dollars and Sense*. This article elaborates on how socioeconomic factors interlink with race, affecting educational outcomes.

Feedback Loops in Race and Opportunity

- Sharkey, P. (2013). *Stuck in Place: Urban Neighborhoods and the End of Progress Toward Racial Equality*. The University of Chicago Press. This book discusses how entrenched socio-economic disadvantages perpetuate cycles of inequality across generations.

Data Challenges and Racial Disparities

- Bennett, M., & McNeal, K. (2020). *Measuring Racial Disparities—A Guide for Data Users*. The National Academies Press. This guide details issues related to racial data collection and interpretation, including gaps and the need for disaggregation.

- Pew Research Center. (2020). "The Link Between Race and COVID-19 Mortality." This report outlines racial disparities in health outcomes, specifically during the COVID-19 pandemic.

Flint Water Crisis
- Mason, K. E. (2017). "The Flint Water Crisis and the Limits of Emergency Management." *Journal of Human Behavior in the Social Environment*, 27(1-2), 16-29. A detailed examination of the administrative decisions leading to the crisis, with an emphasis on systemic neglect of minority needs.
- U.S. Commission on Civil Rights. (2017). "The Flint Water Crisis: A Civil Rights Violation?" This report explicitly connects systematic failures and racial dimensions of governance in Flint.

COVID-19 Impacts
- CDC COVID-19 Response Team. (2020). "Racial and Ethnic Disparities in COVID-19-Related Deaths." *Morbidity and Mortality Weekly Report (MMWR)*, 69(32), 1126-1129. This article provides data about the disproportionate impacts of COVID-19 on different racial groups.
- Cheng, Y., et al. (2020). "Socioeconomic and Health Disparities During the COVID-19 Pandemic." *Health Affairs*, 39(8), 1340-1345. The research illustrates how existing disparities were hampered by institutional neglect.

General Studies on Systemic Racism
- Du Bois, W. E. B. (1903). *The Souls of Black Folk*. This foundational text on racial inequality discusses the structural elements of racism and is still relevant in analyzing current frameworks.
- Kendi, Ibram X. (2019). *How to Be an Antiracist*. One World Publishing. This book addresses systemic racism at every level, providing insights into how to dismantle these enduring structures.

General References on Systemic Racism
- Desmond, M. (2016). *Evicted: Poverty and Profit in the American City*. Crown. This book discusses the intersection of race and economic inequality, emphasizing the systemic structures that perpetuate poverty for communities of color.
- Alexander, M. (2010). *The New Jim Crow: Mass Incarceration in the Age of Colorblindness*. The New Press. Alexander highlights how systemic racism manifests through mass incarceration and its lasting impact on Black communities.
- BCS Research Consortium. (2020). "Racial Disparities in the Criminal Justice System." This report provides statistical evidence of racial discrimination within various facets of the judicial system.

Historical Context and Legislation
- *Brown v. Board of Education*, 347 U.S. 483 (1954). Landmark Supreme Court decision that declared state laws establishing separate public schools for Black and white students unconstitutional.
- *Civil Rights Act of 1964*, Public Law 88-352. A pivotal piece of legislation that outlawed discrimination based on race, color, religion, sex, or national origin.
- *Voting Rights Act of 1965*, Public Law 89-110. This act aimed to eliminate barriers to voting for African Americans, particularly in the Southern states.
- *Fair Housing Act of 1968*, Public Law 90-284. Prohibits discrimination concerning the sale, rental, and financing of housing based on race, color, religion, sex, or national origin.

Grassroots Activism

- Tilly, C., & Tarrow, S. (2015). *Contentious Performances.* Cambridge University Press. Discusses the role of collective action and social movements in creating social change, including civil rights movements.
- Clayton, J. (2016). *Black Lives Matter: The Movement's Origins, Strategies, and Future Potential. American Politics Research.* Analyzes the strategies and implications of the BLM movement as a continuation of past civil rights activism.
- Bey, K. C., & Goh, R. (2020). "Activism in the Age of Technology". *Social Movement Studies.* Examines the influence of social media on modern activist movements like BLM and their global reach.

Supreme Court Decisions Affecting Racism
- *Milliken v. Bradley*, 418 U.S. 717 (1974). A landmark case that limited the ability to mandate school desegregation across district lines.
- *Shelby County v. Holder*, 570 U.S. 529 (2013). Struck down key provisions of the Voting Rights Act, impacting minority voters' access to elections.
- *Students for Fair Admissions v. Harvard*, No. 20-1199 (2023). The court's decision impacts affirmative action policies in higher education admissions.

Statistical Evidence of Racial Disparities
- Pew Research Center. (2021). "Key Facts About Race and Marriage in the U.S." Provides statistics on wealth disparities among racial groups, educational attainment, and employment outcomes.
- Federal Reserve. (2020). "Distribution of Wealth in the U.S. Since 1989." Offers comprehensive data on wealth inequality, highlighting stark contrasts between racial demographics.

Sociological and Psychological Insights
- Bonilla-Silva, E. (2017). *Racism without Racists: Color-Blind Racism and the Persistence of Racial Inequality in America.* Rowman & Littlefield.
  o This text critiques the notion of colorblindness and how it serves to sustain systemic inequality.
- Pager, D. (2003). "The Mark of a Criminal Record." *American Journal of Sociology.*
  o Discusses discrimination in employment based on race and criminal history, emphasizing structural barriers.

Corporate America and DEI Initiatives
- Nishii, L. H., & Mayer, D. M. (2009). "Do Inclusive Leaders Help Embed Inclusiveness in Organizational Culture?" *Journal of Organizational Behavior,* 30(8), 1066-1087.
  o This study examines how inclusive leadership contributes to a culture of inclusivity within organizations.
- Catalyst. (2020). *The Business Case for Diversity: How a Diverse Workforce Can Benefit Your Business.*
  o A report detailing how diverse workforces lead to improved business outcomes, including innovation and financial performance.
- Holvino, E., & Kamp, A. (2009). *Diversity & Inclusion in The Workplace: Key Concepts and Definitions.*
  o This source provides insights into understanding diversity and inclusion in organizational contexts.
- Stevens, M. J., Plaut, V. C., & Sanchez-Burks, J. (2008). "Unlocking the Benefits of Diversity: All-Inclusive Multiculturalism and the Future of Workforce Diversity."
  o This paper discusses strategies companies can adopt to derive maximum benefits from diversity initiatives.

- Williams, J. C., & Dempsey, R. (2014). *What Works for Women at Work: Four Patterns Working Women Need to Know.*
  o This book highlights challenges faced by women, especially women of color, in corporate environments and strategies to overcome these barriers.
- Sullivan, J. (2022). "After Racial Justice Protests, Companies Pledged Billions. Are They Delivering?" *Harvard Business Review.*
  o This article evaluates corporate pledges made in 2020 and assesses whether these actions have resulted in meaningful change.
- Bourke, J., & Dillon, B. (2018). "The Diversity and Inclusion Revolution: Eight Powerful Truths." *Deloitte Insights.*
  o Examines the facts and myths surrounding diversity and argues how inclusive cultures lead to better organizational performance.

Limitations and Critiques
- DiAngelo, R. (2018). *White Fragility: Why It's So Hard for White People to Talk About Racism.* Beacon Press.
  o This book critiques shallow attempts at diversity management and highlights how systemic racism is often obscured in discussions around DEI.
- Kraft, M., & Rose, S. (2023). "The Pitfalls of Diversity Training: A Review of the Evidence." *Shorenstein Center, Harvard Kennedy School.*
  o A detailed review of diversity training effectiveness, emphasizing limitations and potential pitfalls.
- Vaughan, S. (2021). "Corporate Diversity Efforts Under Fire Amid Political Backlash." *Wall Street Journal.*
  o This article addresses the challenges faced by corporations regarding diverse representation amid shifting political landscapes.

The Role of Education in Remediation
- Ladson-Billings, G. (1994). *Toward a Theory of Culturally Relevant Pedagogy.* American Educational Research Journal, 32(3), 465-491.
- Introduces culturally relevant pedagogy and its implications for teaching diverse student populations.
- Banks, J. A. (2010). *Multicultural Education: Characteristics and Goals.* In *Multicultural Education: Issues and Perspectives.*
- Discusses reform in education that incorporates broader perspectives on race and racism through the curriculum.
- Milner, H. R. (2010). *Rac(e)ing to Class: Reflections on Homogeneity and Heterogeneity in Schools and Society.* Urban Education, 45(5), 184-200.
- Highlights the importance of recognizing systemic racism in educational settings and ramifications for student success.
- U.S. Department of Education, Office for Civil Rights. (2014). *Data Snapshot: College and Career Readiness.*
- Discusses disparities in educational opportunities for students of color.
- Parker, L., & Lynn, M. (2002). *What's Race Got to Do with It?* Teachers College Record, 104(7), 1438-1450.
- This article explores the intersections of race and education, focusing on pedagogical approaches that acknowledge systemic inequities.

Policing and Criminal Justice Reform
- American Civil Liberties Union (ACLU). *Smart Justice: An Agenda for Criminal Justice Reform.* 2018. Retrieved from https://www.aclu.org/issues/smart-justice
- National Institute of Justice. *Evidence-based Policing: The State of the Science.* 2020. Retrieved

from https://nij.ojp.gov/library/publications/evidence-based-policing-state-science

Voting Rights
- U.S. Commission on Civil Rights. *An Analysis of Voter ID Laws*. 2018. Retrieved from https://www.usccr.gov/pubs/2018/06-25-VC-Voting-Rights-Table.pdf
- Brennan Center for Justice. *Voting Rights Restoration*. 2021. Retrieved from https://www.brennancenter.org/our-work/research-reports/voting-rights-restoration

Housing Policy
- National Fair Housing Alliance (NFHA). *Fair Housing Trends Report 2019*. 2019. Retrieved from https://nationalfairhousing.org/wp-content/uploads/2020/09/Fair-Housing-Trends-Report-2019.pdf
- Institute for Policy Studies. *The Sustainable Homeownership Program: A Model for Redressing Historic Disinvestment*. 2020. Retrieved from https://ips-dc.org/the-sustainable-homeownership-program/

Educational Equity
- National Center for Education Statistics. *Status and Trends in the Education of Racial and Ethnic Groups*. 2021. Retrieved from https://nces.ed.gov/pubs2021/2021009.pdf
- The Education Trust. *Funding Gaps 2018: An Analysis of School Funding Equity Across the U.S. and Within States*. 2018. Retrieved from https://edtrust.org/resource/funding-gaps-2018/

Economic Opportunity and Wealth Building
- Federal Reserve. (2021). *Report on the Economic Well-Being of U.S. Households in 2020*. Retrieved from https://www.federalreserve.gov/publications/2021-economic-well-being-of-us-households-in-2020.htm
- Darity, W. A., & Mullen, A. K. (2020). *Reparations for Black Americans: A National Policy Proposal*. Faculty Research Working Paper Series. Harvard Kennedy School. Retrieved from https://www.hks.harvard.edu/publications/reparations-black-americans-national-policy-proposal

Healthcare Equity
- National Public Radio (NPR). (2020). *Health Disparities: How Racial Inequity Plays Out in Health Care Performance*. Retrieved from https://www.npr.org/news/2020/07/31/898540854/how-healthcare-inequities-impact-lives-and-longevity-in-the-united-states
- World Health Organization (WHO). (2021). *Social Determinants of Health*. Retrieved from https://www.who.int/health-topics/social-determinants-of-health

General Framework on Systemic Racism
- Kendi, I. X. (2019). *How to Be an Antiracist*. One World.